Tío Cowboy

NUMBER FIVE:
Fronteras Series
Sponsored by Texas A&M International University
José Roberto Juárez, General Editor

Tío Cowboy

Juan Salinas, Rodeo Roper and Horseman

RICARDO D. PALACIOS

Texas A&M University Press
COLLEGE STATION

The paper used in this book meets the minimum requirements
of the American National Standard for Permanence
of Paper for Printed Library Materials, z39.48-1984.
Binding materials have been chosen for durability.
⊗ ♻

Library of Congress Cataloging-in-Publication Data

Palacios, Ricardo D.
Tío cowboy : Juan Salinas, rodeo roper and horseman /
Ricardo D. Palacios. — 1st ed.
p. cm. — (Fronteras series ; no. 5)
Includes index.
ISBN-13: 978-1-58544-527-1 (cloth : alk. paper)
ISBN-10: 1-58544-527-4 (cloth : alk. paper)
1. Salinas, Juan Light, 1901-1995.   2. Rodeo performers—United States—
Biography.   3. Steer roping—United States.   4. Cowboys—United
States—Biography.   5. Mexican Americans—Texas—Biography.
6. Texas—Biography.   I. Title.
GV1833.6.S25P35 2007
791.8′40922—dc22
[B]
2006029385

ISBN-13: 978-1-60344-079-0 (pbk.)
ISBN-10: 1-60344-079-8 (pbk.)

I dedicate this book to all cowboys, the hundreds if not thousands of great cowboys who, unlike Juan Salinas, never got the breaks. This book is also dedicated to the memory of all cowboys who have long ago left us, and to all South Texas cowboys: the best horse trainers, horsemen, and ropers in all of God's little green marble.

Contents

Illustrations

Preface

This is the story of Juan Light Salinas, a South Texas cowboy born and raised in the Brush Country who became a superb calf roper, joined the ranks of the best rodeo performers in the United States, and thus the world, and went where no Mexican had ever been before—and few have gone since. I've set these stories down as I remember them, based on years of listening to my uncle tell and retell the tales of his youth, his years on the professional rodeo circuit, and his life as a South Texas rancher.

Juan Salinas was a big boy, and grew to be a big man. As an adult, at his peak he was 6 feet, 3 inches, and weighed about 250 pounds. He was not a chiseled, muscular man, but he was big in all respects—he had huge bearlike hands, leathery on the inside. He was simply a large person, not fat, but big and very strong. He was a very imposing figure. He was fair, being blond-haired as a child; he had brown hair as an adult, later to turn white, and hazel eyes. He was always a serious, quiet, and reserved person. Although half-Mexican and half-Anglo, he looked Anglo. However, he spoke English with a marked Spanish accent. Even as an adult—after a lifetime of speaking English, having an Anglo mother, going around the United States several dozen times, living with his Anglo wife, and having Anglo friends and family—he spoke in a deep, laconic staccato, with an accent. Of course, to the Mexican population in La Becerra and Encinal, Texas, he was a Mexican, though some called him El Alemán, (the German). He was a man of very few words when working or when in a group of people, until he became familiar with those around him. In a social gathering, he was very quiet at first, then opened up to start talking and telling stories. This is the way I learned all of his stories.

Juan Light Salinas was my *tío*, which means uncle in Spanish. My mother, Mucia, was his sister. Since I was old enough to understand, Tío Juan was the family cowboy, the hero, the rodeo star. We all knew him, we all saw him on occasion, but most of us never were able to visit or talk to him.

Growing up, all I knew was that he had been a rodeo champ, roping calves, and that he had been good enough to make the Championship Rodeo in New York's Madison Square Garden for ten consecutive years, from 1936 to 1946. I saw him rope many times around his ranch near Encinal, Texas.

Rodeo and calf roping in particular has always fascinated me; it is more complicated than meets the eye. First, a cowboy takes a well cared for, and well-trained 1,200- to 1,500-pound horse, he puts a light blanket on him, then a thick saddle blanket. Next, he throws on the saddle, he gets the cinch from one side and runs it through the buckle rings on the other side of the cinch, he keeps running it through and tightening it on each turn until the saddle is on tight. Then, he takes the end of the cinch and puts it through this little leather patch with a slot in it, called the keeper. Then he ties the back cinch, which is loose, just so the saddle is not pulled off the horse from the front by a bull or a strong calf. He puts a thick strap in the front of the horse's breast, called a breast collar, and connects both ends to the D ring on the saddle. This is to prevent the opposite, the saddle from coming off the horse's butt. Then he puts on the headstall, with a noseband. The noseband connects with a small rope or cord to the breast collar, which keeps the horse from rearing back.

The cowboy then puts on the bridle and bit, he puts the bridle over the horse's ears, the bit into the horse's mouth, then he ties the buckle on the side of the bridle. The reins connect to the bridle at the bit. The reins tie together and rest over the saddle horn. The cowboy then ties two 35-foot ropes to the front of the saddle by using the leather ties on the side of the saddle. The cowboy puts on his spurs, his hat, and puts on his pigging string, a 3- to 4-foot rope, looped on one end. The cowboy wears it temporarily like a sash; he puts his head and one shoulder through the loop, tightens it, and tucks it into his belt.

Now the horse is ready. The cowboy mounts, and is ready to warm the horse up, and prepare for the roping. After an hour or so of warm-up, the roper is ready. When the announcer calls his name, he takes off the sash rope, puts a small 8-inch loop in his mouth, and tucks the remainder in his belt. By this time, he has taken out one of the ropes and built a large 6- to 8-foot loop in the roping end of the rope; the rest of the coil he holds in his left hand. The cowboy then rides slowly into the box, next to the chute holding the calf that he will attempt to rope. He slowly backs the horse up to the box, which is roughly about a 10 by 10 pen with one end open to the arena. A rope or rubber barrier crosses the opening of the box, and ties to the chute that holds the calf. When the chute opens to let out the calf, it loosens one end of the barrier, which then permits the roper to run out of the box chasing the calf. If the roper runs through the barrier before it is loosened by the running calf, the cowboy "breaks the barrier," and he is penalized by either a no time, or by adding a penalty, such as 5 or 10 seconds to his time.

When the cowboy quietly backs the horse into the box, the barrier is across the opening of the box, the calf is ready, and the ground hand working the calf chute is looking the roper straight in his eyes. When the cowboy is ready physically and mentally, the horse is ready to take off, and the loop is ready to swing, the roper nods at the ground hand, and the calf is let go, setting off a swift operation, and a time clock.

The cowboy rides the horse at full speed, while he gingerly holds the reins and a 35-foot coil of rope in the left hand he swings the roping loop overhead with the right hand, he chases a 200- to 300-pound calf, and culminates the move by throwing the loop. He ropes the calf, abruptly stops the horse, dismounts, runs toward the calf, grabs the calf, throws it to the ground, pulls the pigging string from his mouth and belt, grabs one front foot, loops it, grabs two hind legs, then ties all three of these to stop the clock and the event.

I asked Juan Light Salinas why area rodeo promoters would come to his ranch near Encinal, in the South Texas Brush Country, to sign him up for rodeos or roping events. I expected him to say that they came because he was an excellent calf roper. Instead, he answered with a deep staccato voice with a slight Spanish accent, "well, not too many peoples seen a Mexican boy throw a loop, so they came to see me. They pay at the gate."

I use the term Mexican because that is the term my uncle used. That is the term my family has always used, and that I have always used. Today there is a tendency to use the term Hispanic or perhaps even Tejano, the Texan Mexican, born in Texas, enveloped by either Spain or Mexico, but very much a Texan, a *Tejano*. In this book, I use the terms interchangeably. We call ourselves Mexican.

From early on my uncle wore a white shirt and khaki pants—a trademark that would distinguish him from others for all of his life. Notwithstanding the obvious Anglo blood, his family considered itself strictly Mexican. Spanish was the language spoken at home and outdoors. Very rarely was English spoken, and then only with his mother, my grandmother, Minnie Light Salinas, whom everyone called Mama Minnie. Mama Minnie herself, 100 percent German Irish, spoke very good country Spanish, and frequently referred to the Anglos in the third person, excluding herself from the group. I remember that occasionally she would say, "*Los Gringos le robaron terreno a Antonio allá cerca de Seguin* (The gringos stole some land from Antonio, over there close to Seguin)." It sounded funny to hear her talk of Anglos as a group of which she was not a part. Of course, when Tío Juan married Tía Bertha, English was necessary, because she did not speak Spanish, but this was only in Tía Bertha's presence.

Tío Juan described a situation to me that coincidentally I have also experienced in my life, that the Anglo will not trust you because you are part Mexican, and the Mexican will not trust you because you are part Anglo. It happens. Not often, but it happens.

Juan Salinas's reference to his celebrity comes from the fact that no other Mexicans were in rodeo at the time. The scarcity of Mexicans in rodeo, and any other activity, was a result of the prejudice and discrimination exercised against Mexicans in Texas and the southwestern states.

Juan Salinas grew up in an era when Mexicans were not served in white-owned restaurants; were severely discriminated against in school and school activities, in business and the work place; and when the separate but equal school system became well entrenched. Even as close as Encinal and Cotulla, there was a white school and a Mexican school. Because of this prejudice it was unlikely that a Mexican could break into professional rodeo.

Regardless of this cultural situation, Juan Salinas and his brother Tony Salinas were able to move about easily. Their competitors and peers loved them, and the love was mutual. They made life-long friendships on the rodeo circuit. Why was this possible? We will never know the answer, but it could be because they were good at their sport, because they were gregarious and unassuming, or because they were good, honest, hardworking cowboys. We will never know for sure, but being Mexican rodeo stars was something completely new and odd, and spectators came to witness the oddity.

What an ironic twist: centuries earlier the Spaniards introduced calf roping, *riatas, chaparreras, espuelas, ranchos,* and everything cowboy, even the very word *rodeo* to the Americas. In the 1930s and 1940s, Juan Salinas, a Spanish descendant Mexican American participating in rodeo, an all-white sport, was the oddity that drew spectators, mostly white, to the rodeo.

Tío Juan's story is also, coincidentally, a story of a people, the Mexican people of South Texas, of the South Texas Brush Country, *la gente del terrenazo* (the people of the big land), as Tejanos call those from South Texas. They were strong, rugged, independent, hard working, confident individuals who repeatedly resisted attacks from the north, and were able to maintain and improve their families, their culture, their property, and their lands. Although some people, like a sociology professor I had at the University of

Texas in Austin in 1962, thought that all Mexicans believed in witchcraft, that all worshiped plaster statues, and other similarly absurd stereotypes, we did not grow up wearing white pajamas and holding straw hats timidly in our hands.

South Texas and Webb County in particular have always been home to a complex society just like any other in the United States. Notwithstanding the fact that the population has usually hovered around 95 percent Mexican American, and perhaps surprisingly to some, there has always been an upper, middle, and lower class socially and economically, there has always been a superb education system, there has always been self governance, law and order, doctors, lawyers, professionals—and many have owned vast tracts of land. Of course, as in any other society, many have been uneducated and poor. Webb County and most of South Texas are just like the rest of the state, the only difference is that the population is mostly Mexican.

Tío Juan was a very fortunate man because he was born of a landed family, and although the wealth was not excessive—he was not a millionaire—he had the land, the cattle, the horses and the assets, and the ability to borrow if need be. His story shows that if you have a talent, regardless of who you are and where you are from, if you work hard and persevere and are tenacious you can succeed. Tío Juan took what he had, improved on it, and ended up in the limelight of the big rodeo arenas of the United States. Tío Juan was a product of this great region called South Texas, the Brush Country, an area where after the Alamo and after the Civil War, Mexicans were able to defend and hold what they had worked hard to earn, and in so doing, to establish themselves as something special, an exception to the rule.

This book is also a tribute to the working cowboy, and the working cattle ranch, both of which are thinning in number year by year, slowly vanishing from the countryside.

Tío Juan was born on the Las Blancas Ranch, the family ranch in northeast Webb County, Texas, in 1901. He took up calf roping from horseback in his early years, and rode his roping skills to all of the major rodeos in the United States, accompanied by his wife, Tía Bertha, until he retired from professional rodeo in 1946. He continued calf roping in area rodeos until the 1960s. He was inducted into the National Cowboy Hall of Fame in Oklahoma City at age ninety, in 1991.

In 1982, my ex-wife and I moved from Laredo, Texas, to a small tract of land 4 miles south of Encinal, Texas. Although I tried to purchase a small tract of land from Tío Juan, he refused, telling me that if he sold me land he would have to sell a small tract to each of his dozens of nephews and nieces. We bought a 60-acre place from someone else, across Interstate 35 from Tío Juan and his wife, my aunt, Tía Bertha. When we first moved to the Encinal area and built our home, Tío and Tía both made it clear that they enjoyed their privacy, and that we should not be pestering them. We understood, respected their wishes, and went about our business setting up our new house, and raising our four children.

As the years went by, Tío and Tía relied on us more and more. We were glad to help. Then in early 1990, Tía Bertha became very ill; she died in April 1991. This meant that Tío Juan, now ninety years old, would need someone to care for him.

He was always so strong and independent that at first we did not understand how much help he needed. It turned out he needed a tremendous amount. He had let Tía Bertha handle all of his problems, but now Tía Bertha was gone. He had put on a good front, but now we knew that he needed help for all necessities. We did as much as we could.

As it turned out, for the next five years I visited with him daily. In fact, I lived with him at his house for two years, and he lived in our house the last two years of his life. Being clear-minded and lucid, having an excellent memory, and being a great storyteller, he began telling stories about his life, the rodeo, and the ranch. Most of the stories came to me in the evening as we watched television. He would talk and talk. Visualize a darkly paneled room, à la 1960s, fire crackling in the fireplace in the distant corner, Tío and I both sitting in recliners, a couple of couches and lamps surround us. A Persian rug covers almost the entire white and gray spotted tile floor. A huge mounted white-tailed deer head hovers above us.

A yellow hue from the incandescent bulbs prevails. To finish out the surroundings, about ten large 3-foot by 4-foot photo frames are filled with a lifetime of rodeo. Action shots, pictures of the important people in his life, Tía Bertha, Toots, brother Tony, pictures of the victories, and the good times complete the collection. I must tell you that I was in awe, and still am in awe every time I look at these photos. I felt like I was in a shrine dedicated to the memory of the rodeo cowboy. It was in this setting that I heard most of Tío Juan's stories.

It turned out to be his life history, detail by detail. I spent evenings and weekends with him listening to stories of his life and his rodeo career as a calf roper, giving me yards and yards of memory-string to save for a later day.

That day has arrived.

I express my appreciation to those who encouraged me repeatedly to keep on writing. To my friend Cynthia Vidaurri, of the Smithsonian Institution, who kept pushing for a Juan Salinas book, and to Dr. Norma Elia Cantú of the University of Texas–San Antonio, who opened the doors to make it happen. I give thanks to those friends and family members who have always liked my storytelling, and encouraged me to put the stories down on paper. My thanks, of course, to the Texas A&M University Press staff for all the help, leading me along to final publication. And, thank you, Lord, for letting me be at least a little bit of a cowboy.

Tío Cowboy

1

Webb County, Texas

Webb County, Texas, lies on the north bank of the Rio Grande, the boundary between the United States and Mexico. The county is in deep southwest Texas, 150 miles south of San Antonio on Interstate Highway 35, and 150 miles due west from Corpus Christi. Laredo is the county seat of Webb County, which is the sixth largest county in the state of Texas and part of what many call the South Texas Brush Country.

Rainfall averages about 20 inches per year, and the countryside consists of gradually sloping hills, the western terminus of the Gulf of Mexico Plains, covered with native brush 6 to 8 feet in height, and mesquite and huisache trees 10 to 20 feet in height. Nopales, prickly pears, cover a large part of the ground. White-tailed deer, feral hog, quail, and other wildlife are plentiful, and rattlesnakes abound. The record books are full of trophy white-tailed deer from Webb County, additions continue annually.

Although the area is semiarid, land along the river is very fertile, being the northern rim of the Rio Grande Valley. With irrigation from the Rio Grande over the last two centuries, the fields have yielded magnificent crops of hay, onion, cabbage, carrots, watermelon, cantaloupe, and many other products. Farming has gone through an evolution that has put the small farmer out of business, but there are still many farms around the Laredo area. Produce comes to Laredo, and after undergoing processing, moves out to the produce markets of the nation. In addition, much produce from Mexico comes through Laredo. Away from the river, the soil varies from gravel hills to red sandy loam to black and gray soil.

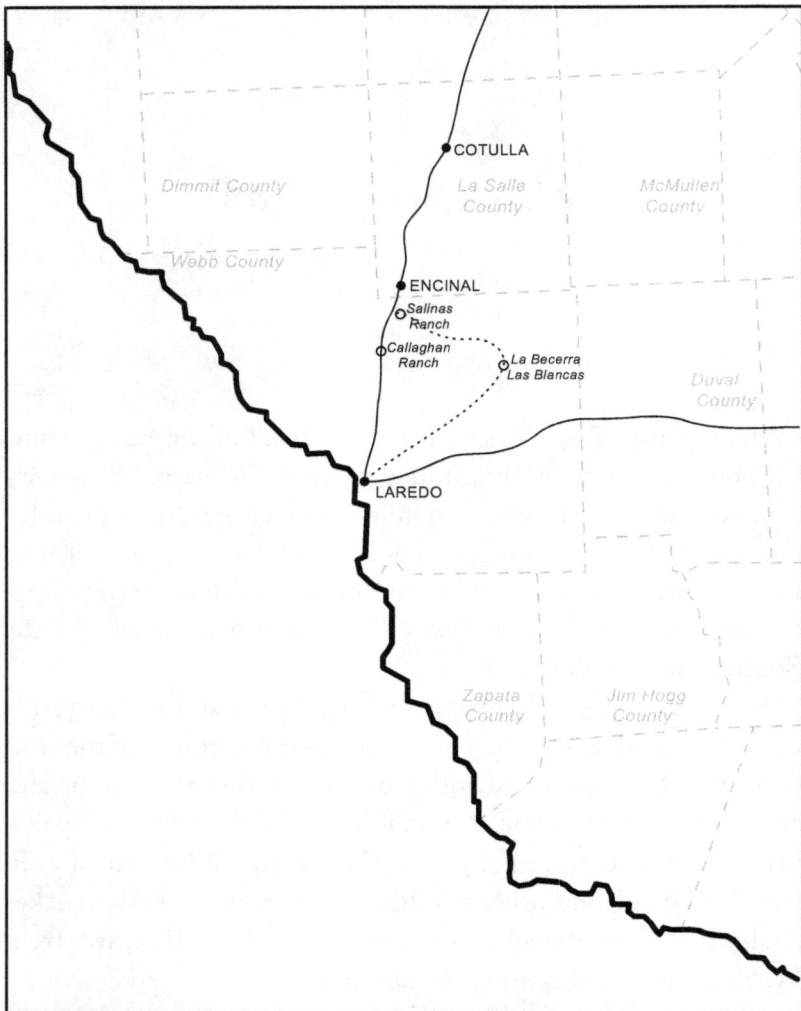

Webb and surrounding counties: the Brush Country

Farmers, whose land does not adjoin the fertile river land, depend on rain for crops.

Cattle producers too must depend on rain for the grass that provides feed for their herds. Many cattle ranchers profess that they raise grass and not cattle. In reality, without the grass, the cattle are insignificant. In dry times cattlemen put out hay that was either raised on their own ranches or purchased and brought in. Although more troublesome, a very effective alternative is to *chamus-*

car, to burn prickly pear. Liquefied natural gas—the propane used in jet burners carried on workers' backs in small backpack models, or 200- to 300-gallon steel tank models on small trailers—burns thorns off the nopales, the prickly pear cactus. The de-thorned, singed cactus is food for the cattle. Neither hay nor burned pear offers much protein, but these maintain the herd until the rains come and provide for grass growth. Even after good rains, it takes weeks for grass and forbs to begin growth, giving rise to the saying, "but it doesn't rain grass." After burning or singeing, the cactus smells like a steamed green vegetable, and the cattle and wildlife cherish it; cattle herd easily with a good burning, or *chamuscada*. In reality, seven or eight years out of ten are very dry, and the cattle and the operation suffer considerably. Drought and the high cost of feed bills discourage many from pursuing an otherwise beautiful and rewarding profession.

In the early 1950s, rancher Arturo T. Benavides from Bruni introduced buffle grass to South Texas, forever changing the countryside. It has been marvelous for this part of the state. Before buffle grass, ranchers depended on sparse native grasses for cattle survival. Buffle grass is extremely hardy, it is full and rich, and makes excellent feed, and most importantly, it spreads like wildfire. Improved buffle grass and other varieties have helped cattle ranchers tremendously. Just about everywhere you turn in South Texas, you see healthy stands of imported grass. Salinas family photos taken in the 1920s, 30s, and 40s show the bare earth, where either native grass stood, or no vegetation grew at all.

Nine months out of the year the temperature is very hot. The temperature soars to the 100-degree Fahrenheit mark during most of the months of June, July, August, and some of September. During much of the rest of the year the temperature hovers in the 90s and high 80s. In November, the temperature drops to the low 40s with highs in the 70s and occasionally in the 80s. December, January, and February lows are mostly in the 40s, sometimes in the 30s, and occasionally in the 20s and teens; highs during these winter months average in the 70s and 80s. Seldom does the temperature drop to freezing or below; if it does, it is only for two or three days. Snow comes but once every twenty years or so, and usually melts when it hits the ground. Sometimes it stays for a day or so, enabling a rare snowman and snowball fight. Any adult can talk of memories of Thanksgiving and Christmas days in the 90s, and some in the hundreds. The year my son Antonio Ignacio was born, 1984, we celebrated Easter Sunday in 110-degree weather.

The founder of Laredo was Don Tomas Sanchez. Laredo was a part of New Spain first, then the Republic of Mexico, then after the Treaty of Guadalupe Hidalgo, a part of the Republic of Texas, and finally, a part of the United States. Laredoans formed their own republic, the Republic of the Rio Grande, that lasted but a couple of months in the 1800s, giving Laredo the added brag of having been under seven flags and not six as the rest of the state.

For the first several years, most of the founding families of Laredo lived on what is now the Texas side of the Rio Grande. In fact, Laredo was the only one of the several villas founded by the Spaniards on the Rio Grande that was established on the north bank. When Laredo became a part of Texas, and the United States, many families moved to the south bank, now the Mexican side of the river, to Nuevo Laredo, Tamaulipas.

History and circumstance have created a microculture along the Rio Grande, centered primarily in Webb County. Unlike other parts of the state, Laredo had little unfriendly immigration after the Civil War, thus preserving its culture, heritage, and wealth. The local Tejanos kept their position through power. My grandfather Antonio Salinas was reputed to have one hundred "yellow boys" at his disposal. "Yellow boys" were .30-30 caliber lever action Winchester rifles of the era; they had a yellow brass action, and thus were nicknamed "yellow boys." To have one hundred yellow boys meant to have one hundred men each armed with a Winchester rifle, and ready to respond if and when necessary. Thus, Hispanics in Laredo and the surrounding counties were able to maintain an upper and middle class, when northern counties were not. In the northern and surrounding counties, most Hispanics lost everything they had. I have met many Texas Hispanics who are in awe of the men and women who come from the South Texas Brush Country—some as leaders, some as just plain individuals, some with a swagger and some not, but all with pride, confidence, and independence. As an example, Webb County produced several of the best and most successful of the Hispanic officers that fought in the American Civil War. Most noted were Colonel Santos Benavides and his brother Captain Refugio Benavides, distant cousins of the Salinases. Descendants of these individuals prosper to this day in Webb and surrounding counties.

In my family, we feel that we inherited our independence and contrarian behavior from the Spanish pioneers. We say that before the discovery of the New World, all the males in Spanish families who were over-confident, independent, rambunctious, over-achievers, and perhaps hyperactive were sent to the haciendas under the supervision of strong and firm *caporales* (foremen). Over-active young men either conformed to acceptable behavior standards or were doomed to live out their lives on the hacienda as cowboys.

After the discovery of the New World, rather than waste the energies on the family hacienda in Spain, the families sought instead to send the young cowboys to the New World, as delegates, in hopes of claiming riches and new land for the family. Thus, some think that the founding families of Laredo, from whom we descend, were mostly hyperactive contrarians who were misfits in Spain and became pioneers to the New World, settling in what would become South Texas. I frequently told my ex-wife that we perpetually swim upriver, against the current. We all laugh about it, but there may be some truth in it.

Today there are very few pure-blooded Spaniards. A pure-blooded Spaniard is a *gachupín*. A Spaniard born in the New World was a *criollo* (creole). At first fine lines distinguished mixtures, such as a *cuarteron*, a *quarteroon*, later those of mixed blood were simply *mestizos*, being part Spanish and part Mexican Indian.

Today we are mostly mixed. More than any other border area, Laredo has been a true melting pot of ethnic groups. Hungarians, Polish and Russian Jews, Germans, Italians, French, Lebanese, Greeks, and many others have readily settled in the Laredo area and eventually mixed with the predominant Spanish and Mexican Indian. Today most of us are simply *encartados*, of mixed blood, presenting a beautiful spectrum of color, varying from dark ebony or coffee, to brown, to golden brown, to gold, *cafe con leche* (coffee with milk), to whitest of the white. Our eyes range from the very dark brown through light brown, hazel, green, and blue to the light blue-white. Today as citizens of this great country, we consider ourselves Americans first and above all, whether our heritage is Mexican, Spanish, Italian, French, Polish, German, Lebanese, Greek, or whatever. I know from family history that during the early decades, national origin, or ethnic origin, did not play a big part in the life of the Salinases. The important things were to be unbothered, to fend for themselves, survive, and make a living.

There are those in the family who say that we are pure-blooded Spaniards, but I find it hard to believe that the Spaniards who conquered Mexico City and then took over two hundred years to arrive at what is now Laredo did not intermarry with the natives. I guess that only when the genome is finished will we be able to tell for sure. When the Spaniards arrived in Laredo they were probably already of mixed blood. Our family has been here from the beginning.

The first contingent of Spanish settlers arrived on the north bank of the Rio Grande at what is now Laredo, Texas, in 1755, 236 years after Cortez conquered the Aztecs in Mexico City. They named the river and the settlement they founded. The river they called Big River, Rio Grande; they also called it the Rio Bravo, which means Fierce or Vicious River, not literally translated as the Brave River, as some say. After crossing the river, they named the settlement Laredo, after a city in the province of Santander in Spain by the same name. The Spaniards knew the area as Nuevo (New), Santander.

When the Spaniards arrived, they brought an entire industry with them: the cattle industry. They brought the cattle, and they brought the horses to work them. Of course, they brought the technology, a whole system of equipment, technique, and craft for working the cattle. Several decades after arrival, the cattle population had spread to the entire area later to be the state of Texas. With the increase in population came the advent of the rancho or hacienda, the cattle ranch, largely imitating the ranches and haciendas in Spain.

2

The Antonio Salinas Family
of Webb County, Texas

One of the descendants of Spaniards who became a prominent citizen of Laredo was Bartolome Garcia, the great-great-grandchild of Don Tomas Sanchez, the city's founder. Bartolome, sometimes also referred to as Bartolo, married Maria del Carmen Benavides in 1833. One of Bartolome's largest contributions—literally—to the growth of Laredo was the fact that he had twelve children. Descendants of these became foundation families of Laredo and today descendants of these prevail in large numbers. One of the ten children was Mucia Garcia. Mucia Garcia married Juan Francisco Salinas. They had five children, Antonio Salinas, his sisters, Margarita, Inocente, Teresa, and Maria. Antonio Salinas was my grandfather, and the father of Juan Light Salinas. Antonio became a businessman, cattle rancher, and politician. He was a hard and sometimes very harsh man. Jerry Thompson, in *Warm Weather and Bad Whiskey: The 1886 Laredo Election Riot*, a history of the political feuds in Laredo at the end of the century, reports that during the battle on the Plaza San Agustin, Antonio Salinas announced, *"Ya mate al Gringo"* ("I have killed the gringo"). He spoke of having taken one Whitley to the bank of the Rio Grande and killing him with pistol shot. He never stood trial for the killing. Antonio (called Papá Antonio by our family), received a bullet wound in the abdomen in that riot, and underwent surgery. Years later, a suspender button from his pants exited his abdomen through the surgical scar. Apparently, the bullet hit the button and it stayed in his abdomen during surgery. Family history has it that on another occasion he took an employee's eye out with a horsewhip. Family

Captain Tomas Sanchez / Catalina Uribe
Had a Great Grandson

Bartolome Garcia / Maria del Carmen Benavides
Born 1813
Great Grandson of
Captain Sanchez

They Had Twelve Children

Cesareo / Genoveva Rodriguez	Margarita (Nun)
Paula / Agustin Salinas	Maria Refugio / Lazaro de la Garza
Isidro	Julian / Esther Borrego
Luisa	Leonides
Jose Maria / Cresencia Ramon	Rosendo
Tirza / Raymond Martin	

And

Mucia Garcia   *Married*   Juan Francisco Javier Salinas
Born 1835   *Born 1834*

They Had Five Children

Margarita	Teresa / D.Z. de la Chica
Inocente	Maria / Francisco Guerra

And

Antonio Salinas
1858-1923
Married Twice

Maria Garcia   Minnie Light (1881 - 1951)

Mother Of   *Mother Of*

Antonio	***Juan Light Salinas*** / Bertha Hargraves
Jose Alberto	Jose Maria Salinas / Blanca Cisneros
Lucinda	Mucia Salinas Palacios / Abe Palacios
	Margarita Salinas Rubio / Enrique Rubio
	Antonio Light Salinas (Tony) / Lucille Juvenal

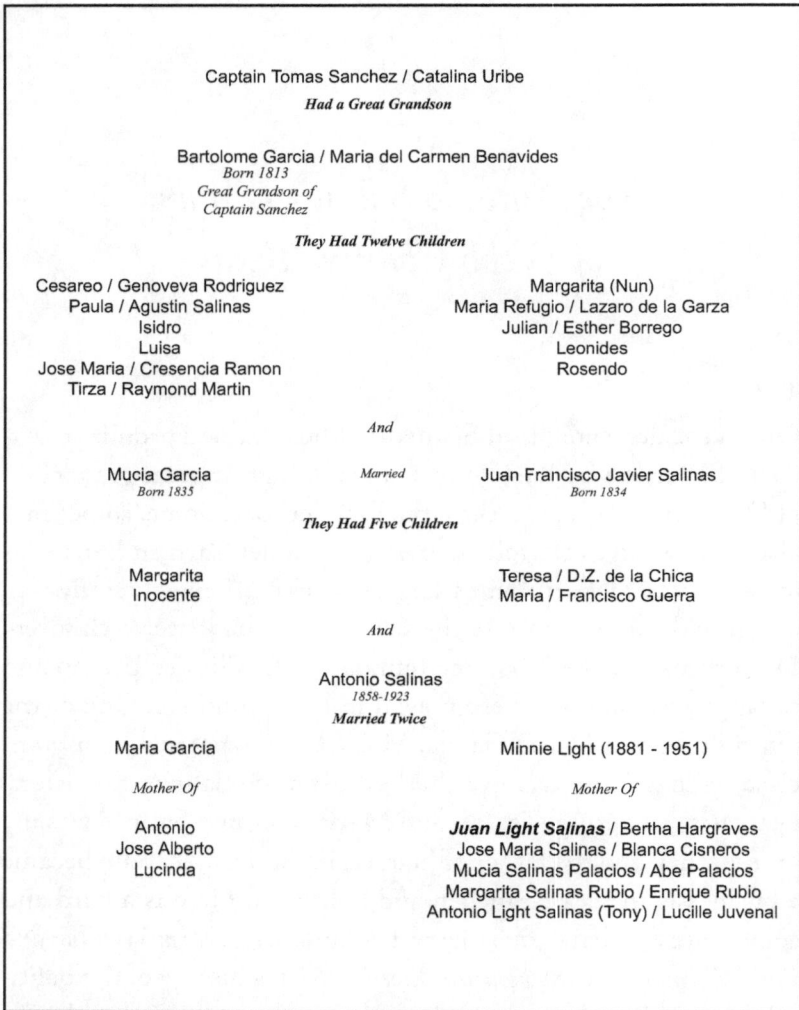

Abridged family tree: Juan Light Salinas

history also has it that he rarely smiled, one remembered occasion being on the birth of his first grandson, Carlos Salinas. Notwithstanding his apparent harshness and violent character, having the right family connections, Papá Antonio became sheriff of Webb County in the early 1920s. The inventory filed in the probate case of Papá Antonio's estate shows that he had about 15,000 acres of land, although after his death, half of it was sold to pay debt. Even

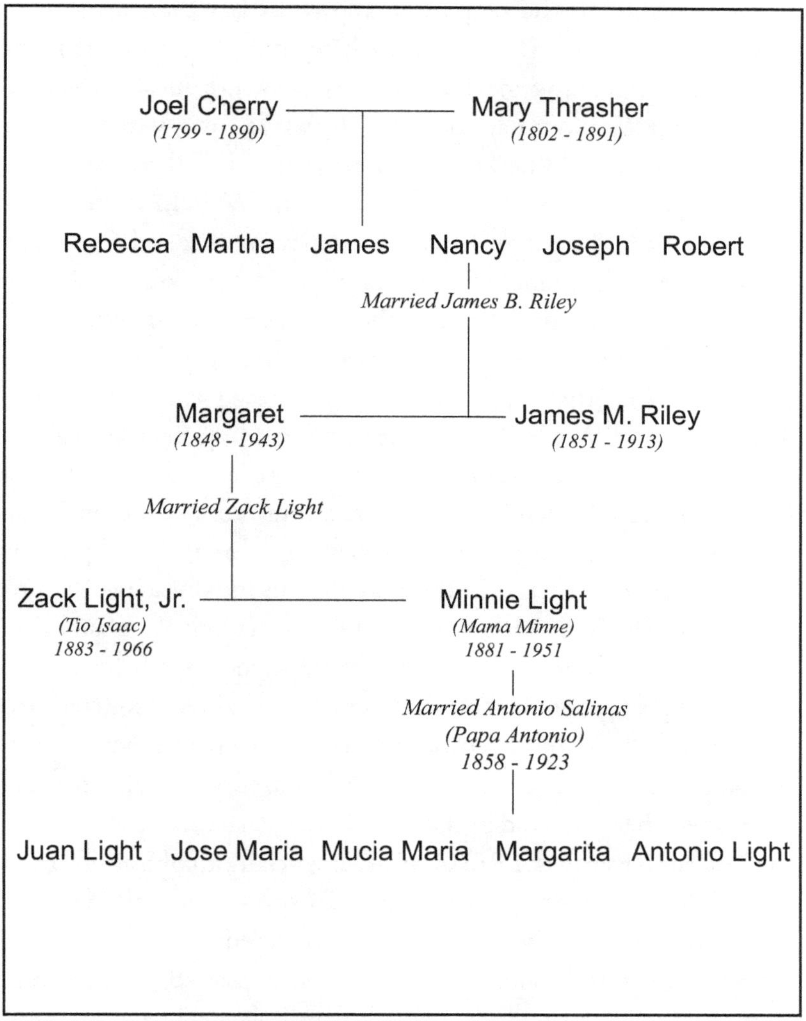

Joel Cherry ———————— Mary Thrasher
(1799 - 1890)   *(1802 - 1891)*

Rebecca   Martha   James   Nancy   Joseph   Robert

Married James B. Riley

Margaret ———————— James M. Riley
(1848 - 1943)   *(1851 - 1913)*

Married Zack Light

Zack Light, Jr. ———————— Minnie Light
(Tio Isaac)   *(Mama Minne)*
1883 - 1966   *1881 - 1951*

Married Antonio Salinas
(Papa Antonio)
1858 - 1923

Juan Light   Jose Maria   Mucia Maria   Margarita   Antonio Light

Abridged family tree: Minnie Light Salinas

in the early times, the toil of running a cattle operation proved very difficult, even more so with raising a family of six, one day's ride from Laredo.

In the late 1800s Antonio acquired substantial acreage in northeast Webb County: the ranch, totaling about 14,000 acres. It is about 45 miles northeast of Laredo. Today it, or part of it, is the Williamson Ranch; it used to be the Lincoln Ranch. When Papá

Antonio owned it, the ranch was known as Las Blancas, it is located in the Becerra (Heifer), Ranch region. Origin of the name
Las Blancas is lost to time, but it means the white ones, in the feminine gender. Could it have been for the white cows, white hills, or
the white women? Who knows? When Antonio Salinas moved to
the Encinal area, he sold Las Blancas to one W. P. Lincoln. Those
who were born, raised, or lived in that area were called *becerreños*.
These include the Donato Guerra family, the Aguirres, the Adam-
ses, the Hinojosas, and of course the Salinases, among others. The
number of living becerreños has dwindled to a very few.

By the time that Papá Antonio purchased the Las Blancas
Ranch, most of Webb County was cattle country. Scattered about
the county there were established communities called ranchos or
haciendas. Each hacienda consisted of a community of several families living together in a small area that served as the headquarters
of a large ranch, usually in the many thousands of acres. It took
decades for the Spaniards to settle the countryside after establishing the village of Laredo. Native Americans who already lived there
contested possession. It took about one hundred years for the haciendas to take hold, but once established they were microcultures of
the larger cities a distance away, such as Laredo. The violence and
bloodshed that occurred in the Nueces Strip, the area of land from
the Nueces River to the Rio Grande, essentially all of South Texas,
affected the ranchos and haciendas. In some cases, the violence
caused the abandonment and retreat to Laredo. It was not until
after the 1880s and 1890s, after the violence quieted, that the ranchos and haciendas once again took firm hold in the countryside.

In each of the haciendas were people who had acquired all of the
skills brought over from Europe by the Spaniards. Although not
affluent by any means, each hacienda was self-sufficient. The technology, techniques, skills, and the entire system of survival brought
by the Spaniards two centuries earlier, survived on the haciendas,
at least into the first third of the twentieth century—and some of
these techniques survive to this date. Each hacienda had one or
more workers skilled in working with leather. They wove strips of
leather into ropes (*riatas*), or into whips (*chicotes*), and they made

chaparreras (chaps), *monturas* (saddles), *cinchos* (cinches), *pecho pretales* (breast collars), *jacimas* (hackamores), *bosales* (headstalls), *riendas* (reins), and anything else required for the horses, and for working cattle.

Barbed wire did not exist yet. Squeeze chutes, freeze branding, and huge pick-up trucks were still decades away. Largely, the fence as we know it today did not exist. For working pens at the ranch headquarters, the ranchers built *corrales de leña* (pens made from mesquite wood). Several straight mesquite poles were stuck vertically into the ground about 2 feet deep, in two rows 2 feet apart, and mesquite wood was laid horizontally between the poles and tied with whatever material was available. If there was nothing to tie with, the weight and gravitational pull on the wood sufficed, and the vertical poles were planted closer together. This mass of wood formed a log wall, and these walls were formed in whatever configuration was necessary to work the cattle and horses of the hacienda. To this date, the Juan Salinas Ranch 3 miles south of Encinal, has an excellent set of antique corrales de leña, built about one hundred years ago, and maintained through the decades with fresh vertical poles and fill-in mesquite wood.

Ancient Spanish records show that the Spaniards designated their livestock as either small (*ganado menór*), or larger livestock (*ganado mayór*). At each hacienda were plenty of *ganado menór*—goats, chickens, guineas, and the like, for food purposes.

Someone was always making butter and cheese, and there were plenty of white-tailed deer available for making venison and *carne seca* (jerky). I have heard or read that the Comanches called venison God's meat, because it has always been so plentiful and available. There were plenty of collared peccary, or *javalines* (javelinas). Tío Juan and his good friend Ramon Flores joked about javalines. They do not have a tail, and the story goes this way: "One year it got so cold, it went down to about zero degrees. It was so cold that the javalines dug holes and buried themselves in the holes. The only thing sticking out of the hole was their tails. Then the people went out and tried to get all the javalines out of the holes for food, and their tails broke off. Thereafter, all javalines ran around without tails, they never grew tails again. That is the legend of how javalines lost their tails."

The hacienda always had people who were skilled in making clothing, in building edifices and fences, and in making shades and shacks. A sturdy *sombra* (shade), made out of South Texas black brush that is good for little else, can be built by applying skills brought from the old country. To make a sombra, long bunches of dry brush are stacked side by side and fastened with wire or rope on top of a trellis made from mesquite poles.

The stage of the moon controlled most everything that took place on the ranch, such as castration, planting, slaughtering, and even chopping wood for use in buildings. A fence post chopped and trimmed when the moon is waning will rot and suffer bug infestation within the year. A fence post chopped and trimmed when the moon is waxing will last forty or fifty years. Mesquite wood is the best and hardest wood and is excellent for cooking, building, and warmth, while huisache is not good for much, besides a campfire.

Most people on the ranch were skilled de facto meteorologists, gifted in predicting the weather. High yellow clouds in the distance meant a hailstorm. Turtle or snakes on a roadway meant imminent rain. Cattle lying down meant a sure change in the weather. Animals out for a late evening feeding frenzy meant a norther would soon blow in. The cenizo bush blooming with purple flowers meant rain was sure to come. Heavy fruit on mesquite trees, huisache trees, and cactus meant that a drought was on or was sure to come in the following months. Tío Juan also talked about the *cabañuelas*. Since time immemorial, we Mexicans have used the cabañuelas to predict the annual weather, by the weather on the first twelve days of the year. Each day represents a month. As an example, if January 3 is a rainy day, that means that March, the third month of the year will be a wet month, and so on. There are variations and extensions of the cabañuelas, superimposing the second set of twelve days over the first, and then going until the end of January, then backing up. It can get out of hand actually. I guess you could say the cabañuelas are about as reliable as a farmer's almanac in predicting the weather. These may be very reliable, or very erroneous.

Aside from the skills and techniques practiced on the ranch inherited from the Spaniards, new ideas and technology developed out of necessity. The workers became de facto engineers, veterinarians, carpenters, doctors, pharmacists, dieticians, *parteras* (midwives), seamstresses, shoemakers, agronomists, and were skilled in any art or science. Gradually mass production in factories at nearby villages or towns eliminated certain roles on the ranch. For example, after the passage of several decades, manufacture of shoes, boots, and clothing moved to the city. Eventual migration played a part, as a skilled cobbler or tailor can make a better living in the city than in a sparsely populated ranch area.

To show off his ability with numbers Tío Juan would sometimes rattle off, as if reading poetry, in meter, "there are five thousand two hundred and fifty feet in a mile, there are forty three thousand five hundred and sixty square feet in an acre, there are six hundred and forty acres in a section of land, a section of land is one square mile, there are sixteen and a half feet in a rod, and there are 2.77 feet in a Mexican vara, a street block in Laredo is one hundred Mexican varas, or 277 feet, there are three feet in a yard, twelve inches in a foot, and sixteen sixteenths in an inch." Then he smiled proudly.

Tío Juan explained to me that he learned how to castrate livestock as a young man, and that there were different techniques in doing horse, cattle, goats, and pigs. Each had a slightly different step to take. He also explained that the goat herders had a special way of castrating baby goats. The goatherd picked up the baby goat and held it in front of his face, he then placed the scrotum, the little sack that holds the testicles, inside his mouth, resting on his tongue. He then scissored left and right with the edge of his front teeth bottom and top, severing the vas, without cutting the skin, the equivalent of a vasectomy.

Lumber, steel, and iron were not available. Consequently, in order to make a gate, ingenuity created what we know today as a *falcete*, a wire gap. A few strands of wire or leather rope stretch across a fence opening. Four or five wood staves stand vertically in the opening tied to the horizontal strands of wire or leather. The ends of the rope or wire consist of small or thin wooden posts. The thin post on one end ties to the existing fence. The falcete closes by placing the other thin post into a loop on the bottom of the fence, and closes with a fulcrum lever at the top of the fence, slipped into another wire loop. Ingenuity and physics created a gate.

A resource used extensively was *cuero* (rawhide), not only to tie fences but also to tie just about anything that needed tying. A rope made of cuero also served as a length for measure. A surveyor used a certain length of leather rope for linear measure, for a survey, or for laying out a building site. Later, metal chains made the leather rope obsolete. Today, surveyors use high-tech satellite equipment. I have heard that many ancient surveys of ranches are inexact because of the use of leather ropes. The survey crew would be out for weeks at a time surveying a large ranch. In the evening, the leather ropes, left in the open, were subject to exposure to dew or rain. The following morning the crew would use the leather ropes and stretch them for measuring. The wet or moist leather would stretch beyond its dry length, thus causing errors in measurement. Rawhide was also used to make ropes and all horse equipment, saddles, *tapaderas* (stirrup covers), *maneas* (hobbles), and it was used in construction to bind beams.

At about the turn of the century, a woman and two children appeared at the Las Blancas Ranch, brought there by neighbors. The woman was looking for work for herself and her daughter and son. The woman was Margaret Riley (later to become my great-grandmother), her daughter was Minnie Light (later to become my grandmother), and the son was Zack Light Jr. Asked why her name was not Light, she replied that Zack Light had treated her badly, that he abandoned her, and that he was a rambunctious no-good, causing her to drop his name. She preferred to use her maiden name, Riley. They mentioned they were German Irish from the Texas Hill Country, but did not elaborate, and no one questioned them further.

Margaret Riley died at the Salinas Ranch in 1943, at the age of ninety-five, and her body rests at the cemetery in Encinal. For years, this was all anyone knew about my great-grandmother. Our genealogical darkness went on until 2001. Then, by pure coincidence, in one week we gained a hundred years of history.

My cousin Henry Rubio lives in Dallas. He belongs to a cowboy action shooting organization called a single action shooting society. Henry took our Tío Zack's (and our great-grandfather's) name as a "stage" name—Lightnin' Zack Light. Jim Gray, from Kansas, who calls himself The Cowboy, has a monthly newspaper and writes about the shooting events and some historical matters. He noticed the name Zack Light in a report on a contest, then called Henry and wanted to know where he got the name. Henry explained. Jim Gray sent Henry several historical articles about Zack Light written by Robert Yarmer. It seemed Zack's father was a Yankee soldier from New York who had made his way to Texas after the Civil War. Zack became a cattle driver on the cross-country cattle drives, and later was in the cattle business. The stories put Zack as close to us as Pearsall, Texas, about 70 miles from Encinal. We read the articles, and it sure sounded like it could be the same person as our unsavory ancestor. The dates were right, and what were the odds of two cowboys by the name of Zack Light about the same time in history, in the same part of the country? The last story said he was killed in a gunfight in 1890. Still, we could not be sure.

Upon further investigation, we discovered that Yarmer's wife was a descendant of Zack Light's sister, Nettie. Not only that, but Mrs. Yarmer had Nettie's Bible. Gray suggested we obtain a book by Harold Hutton, *Doc Middleton: Life and Legends of the Notorious Plains Outlaw*. The book contained a great deal of information about our Riley ancestors, including the fact that the subject of the book, Doc Middleton, was really the same person as James Riley, the brother of our great-grandmother, Margaret Riley. The book further stated that Margaret married Zack Light and had two children, named Minnie and Zack—my grandmother and great-uncle. My mother corroborated all these facts in a recorded interview she gave to my cousin, Margie Rubio, about six months prior to her death.

Meanwhile, back at the Salinas Ranch in the early 1900s. . . . As it turned out, Antonio and Minnie Light, the daughter of Margaret Riley, fell in love, and before long, they had a family. Juan Light Salinas was born in 1901, Jose Maria Salinas in 1903, Maria Mucia

Minnie Light Salinas

Salinas (my mother), was born in 1906, Margarita Salinas in 1908, and Antonio Light Salinas in 1911. All the children were born at the Rancho Las Blancas. Papá Antonio provided a medical doctor from Laredo for each of the births.

Antonio G. Salinas

It was not until 1920, when Tony (as Antonio the younger was called), was ten years old, and at the insistence of Papá Antonio's spinster sisters, Inocente and Margarita, that Papá Antonio decided it would be best to marry Minnie, who by then was called Mamá Minnie. They married at San Agustin Catholic Church (now the cathedral) on the plaza in Laredo in 1920.

As with most children raised on a farm or ranch, the Salinas children flourished in the ranch environment. In later conversations with Tío Juan, he related that the La Becerra community was a self-contained village, having a grocery store, a butcher shop, a barber, a visiting pharmacist or druggist, and a visiting priest. Celebration of holidays brought people from the surrounding ranches and from Laredo. He said most holidays were two- or three-day affairs.

When the Salinas children reached school age, during the school year they were moved to Laredo to live with Tía Chente (Inocente) and Tía Margarita in their house on Lincoln Street in downtown Laredo. During holidays and the summer recess they returned to the ranch and Mamá Minnie. All of the children continued this routine until the girls graduated from high school and elected to stay in Laredo with the aunts, to continue their studies or to work.

Momma told me that her brother Chema was a very intelligent and dynamic man. His progeny has exhibited this trait. His granddaughter is Elma Salinas Ender, a state district judge in Laredo. Chema's oldest son Carlos Salinas went from college straight to piloting bombers during World War II. After many years in the military, he became a teacher. At East Texas State College, now University, Carlos was on a blazing 440-yard relay team that captured victory at most track meets, including the Kansas Relays and the Drake Relays. Carlos, Alfonso Valls from Laredo, Mike Mercado, and Angel Coronado were known in track circles as "The Latin Quartet." In 1948, Carlos ran one of the fastest times in the nation in the 220-yard dash. Carlos's brother Oscar, the Judge's father, was a bombardier during World War II and fought in the Pacific theater. The third son Manuel went to Baylor Dental School. Carlos resigned from the Army Air Corp as a lieutenant colonel. Oscar went to college and became a chemical engineer.

Tío Chema was an excellent shot with a pistol, rifle, or shotgun. He could shoot anything thrown in the air, and he would wait for game to run, and then take a shot to kill, finding this more challenging than a stationary target. Although he dropped out of school early, he frequently helped Momma and Tía Maggie with

Juan Light Salinas as a teenager, ca. 1913

their trigonometry, geometry, and algebra homework. His love was agronomy, growing plants and vegetables would be his livelihood, and his career ended as a large-scale planter in southern Mexico.

Juan, in contrast, at age seventeen begged his father to let him drop out of school so he could devote all of his time to cowboying on the ranch. After many pleas, Papá Antonio relented, only if Juan attended a business school in Laredo. Tío went to a school owned by a Professor Naranjo, and attended Holding Institute, a Methodist Church school that accepted boarders. I have his graduation certificate, which is an interesting piece of history in itself. It is a formal diploma from Draughon's Practical Business College, issued through Holding Institute, Laredo, Texas, dated May 1, 1919. It lists the courses and the grades: Bookkeeping 98, Banking 85, Penmanship 95, Commercial Arithmetic 85, Commercial Law 85, Business Grammar 80, Business Letter Writing 80, Spelling 90, and Deportment 90. After completing his studies, Tío was free to stay on the ranch and work.

My mother, Mucia Salinas Palacios told me that Papá Antonio usually drove a small one-horse express buggy out to Las Blancas and back to Laredo; the one-way trip took one day. During all this time, Papá Antonio kept driving back and forth to Laredo. Momma told me that on a trip back to Laredo, Indians began to follow him. He had to hurry, bury his money, and ride back to the ranch for help. Momma spoke of a couple of Indian attacks at the Las Blancas. She described the raids as not being quite as violent or as loud as shown in the movies. To her they were a large group of dark men that approached the main ranch, and rode off with horses or cattle. There was no gunfire, and she said that the ranch employees got horses, weapons, formed a posse, and chased the Indians until they recovered the stolen livestock.

Tío Juan and his good friend Ramon Flores told me about the migration of Indians around the turn of the century. The Indians came through like the ducks or geese, going south at the first sign of cold weather. Tío said they were not friendly and came into town only to buy supplies. Ramon commented to me that they looked vicious and savage, and he said he would hate to have to fight one; it would be like fighting hand to hand with a *javalin* (javelina).

Momma spoke of the meager existence at Las Blancas and in Laredo. Those were not affluent times. Mom says they did not have much at all by way of material things, one or two changes of clothes, as an example. Mom described life with Mamá Minnie at Las Blancas, and I witnessed the same during my visits to the Salinas Ranch near Encinal in the 1950s. Mamá Minnie was a very quiet person, a trait Tío Juan inherited from her. She mostly spoke in Spanish. Her kitchen was sparse, and her cooking very bland and simple. Meat and potatoes and pinto beans with flour tortillas were about it without much variety.

Momma Mucia inherited the same bland cooking style. I did not start eating spicy salsa, vegetables, and other spices, until I left to go to college. Momma's was not a Mexican kitchen. I can recall in my lifetime that she made *tamales* once or twice, and the same for *menudo*. Even Mom's *picadillo* (sautéed hamburger), usually with lots of spices—*chile, tomate y cebolla*—was bland and unaccompanied by anything other than garlic powder and maybe a chopped bell pepper. Notwithstanding the simplicity of the cooking, one recipe made it through the passage of time—meat turkey dressing, with pecans, almonds, raisins, boiled egg, toasted bread, olives, and other ingredients. Luckily, I learned the recipe from Momma Mucia, and cook it regularly at Thanksgiving and Christmas.

Thus, from this rare mix of chemistry, Juan Salinas had everything that enabled him to develop into a cowboy, in the truest sense of the word, and into a champion caliber rodeo star—he had his family and their love, all the ranch land one would ever need, excellent horses, cattle, and old cowboys to teach him. Anytime you see a rodeo star, somewhere in his past or history is a wise old cowboy who taught him the ropes. Juan had no idea he would be in American rodeo as one of its stars. In fact, Juan did not realize he would be in national rodeo until he was already in it, in his thirties.

Aside from producing beef, the ranch also produced mesquite firewood. There was no natural gas in Laredo at the time, and each household heated and cooked with mesquite. Thus, there were always stacks and stacks of mesquite poles around the ranch, stockpiled for used on the ranch, or waiting for sale to firewood dealers in Laredo. Today, mesquite wood still sells on some ranches. In Laredo, it transforms into small bundles of firewood, or mesquite charcoal, or fuel in Nuevo Laredo, Mexico, for the brick factory kilns. The late Laredo attorney Philip Kazen used to say that we should build a monument to the mesquite tree in Laredo, to honor the tree for its huge contribution to life in Laredo, and to domestic and international commerce.

Times were usually hard, and the Salinases were always looking out for other ways to make money. As a matter of fact, Tío said the only reason he took off on the national rodeo circuit was money. Earnings from the ranch provided very little money. Tío had many cousins in Laredo, and on one of our Sunday drives he told me about a very ambitious cousin. The cousin had a surefire way to make a lot of money.

"It was during prohibition. There was no liquor, and this *primo* (cousin), he decided he could find a way to get rich. He went into Mexico to make some contacts. Soon he became a big *contrabandista*, bringing in liquor as *contrabando* (contraband).

"We all knew it was illegal, but nobody thought it was that serious, it was just whiskey. This cousin he kept on going, smuggling more and more tequila and whiskey. We was close, so I knew exactly what he was doing and how he was doing it.

"Sure enough, one day he got caught. Good thing he was caught by the Texas police, and not by the *federales*. He was in jail, and he sent for me, he asked me to post bail so he could get out and wait for his trial. I knew him, and I trusted him, he was my cousin, so I signed a bail bond for $50,000. He was to go to trial in one month.

"As the time for trial got near, the cousin realized that he was not going to be able to beat the charge, because he was caught with a big load.

"Well wouldn't you know it, I got word one week before trial that my cousin had skipped to Mexico and was not coming back. This meant I was going to have to come up with $50,000 cash to pay the bond, something that was impossible, unless I sold the entire ranch. Not knowing what to do, I go to see Tío Juanito Martin. Tío Juanito was shocked that our cousin would go to Mexico and leave me hanging."

"He can't do that, he'll ruin you," said Tío Juanito. "Where is he?" he asked.

"I told Tío Juanito that the cousin was in Mexico, and Tío Juanito insisted that I go find him and bring him to Tío Juanito. So I did. Tío Juanito and most of our older cousins were powerful politicians. Papá Antonio had been one of the strongest members of their political party, so they felt they knew how to take care of the problem. Tío Juanito told the cousin that he had already talked to the district attorney, and to the judge, and that it was fixed, the cousin would get three years, and be home in eighteen months, and he would get trustee duty at the prison in Huntsville.

"After thinking about it, the cousin thought it was a good deal, and agreed to accept the deal, provided that I, who was about to lose $50,000, would take care of his wife and kids. Boy that was something I didn't want to do, but he says that if I don't take care of the wife and kids, that he skips to Mexico, so I don't have no choice.

"I kept them at the Salinas Ranch here in Encinal, and the cousin he had a good time. He was home on furlough every sixty days, and during hunting season he would be at the ranch every other weekend, with all the big shots, wardens, and guards from Huntsville. They loved to come to Laredo to go to Boys Town across the river, and eat and get drunk, then come out to the ranch during the day and hunt. They set up a camp close to the headquarters, and they loved it.

"I was glad when the eighteen months was up, then the cousin he come and get his wife and kids, and of course, he was mad at me because I did not take good care of his wife and kids." No telling what the wife told him.

Tío never said it, but in reading between the lines, I suspected that Tío was the one who put up the money for the illegal venture. Lucky for him, he did not have to do the time.

The other income source on the ranch came after World War II. With affluence, and more time for outdoor activity, the ranks of hunters increased tremendously. Hunters needed places to go hunt, and they ended up coming to South Texas to get where the *cacaistes* (big mossy backs), live. This gradually grew into a billion-dollar industry. At first hunters were able to hunt for free, or next to nothing. Then landowners started leasing or renting their land to hunters for the deer season. Today this is the prevalent way to rent land. Hunters pay a fee on a per gun basis, to hunt on a ranch during the white-tailed deer season. My childhood mentor, Hi Goodwin, told me that after World War II he went hunting just about wherever he wanted in Webb and Zaptata counties. He went to one small rancher frequently, and the price of the hunt was a loaf of white, thin-sliced bread, something new at the time, that the rancher did not get often.

Tío told me an interesting story about killing a doe when it was still against the law. "My brother Chema and a group of his friends came up from Laredo to hunt deer. They hunted all day and did not see any bucks, and they decided that if they did not kill that afternoon, they would go headlighting, which was also illegal. Headlighting is simply hunting at night with a spotlight. Deer are much easier to kill at night when they cannot see, and their eyes shine when the light hits them. They went headlighting and could not find a buck, so decided to shoot a doe. They shot it, field dressed it, and carried it to camp, where it was hung on a mesquite tree. In the morning, the hunters were asleep when suddenly the game warden drove up and found the evidence. The game warden was a good one, because he was always making arrests, I forget his name, but he had a wooden leg, and he was fierce, everybody was afraid of him. The game warden woke up all the hunters and took them in to Encinal to charge them before the justice of the peace. He made them put the doe in his car trunk. Well, it turned out that the justice of the peace was out of town, so the game warden made the hunters string up the doe on a tree at the justice of the peace's house, and told them to come back for trial the next day. During the day the hunters went out and shot a six-point buck, they tagged it as required by law, waited until dark, then drove to Encinal and switched the evidence, they took the doe and left the six-point buck.

"The following day, everyone showed up for trial, and the game warden was extremely angry because he realized he had lost his case. The judge could not proceed without evidence. The hunters they just looked around at each other fighting like hell to keep from laughing. Finally, the judge told them they could leave. They got fierce warning from the judge and the game warden."

Tío Juan was no exception in using the ranch to produce additional revenue from hunting. Tío only had two hunter's rules that he cared to enforce. "I don't allow no womens, and I don't allow no motorcycles. If they bring womens, first thing you know they get drunked up, then they start fighting over the womens, and I don't want no trouble like that. Then if they bring motorcycles, they make lots of noise, then the deer all run off, then they start telling lies that Juan Salinas don't have no deer. No, no, no womens and no motorcycles."

"During the depression I used to sell deer," Tío Juan told me one day. "Things were very tight, and there was no money anywhere for anybody. There was this fellow from San Antonio used to come down here hunting every year, and he told me he would buy all the buck deer I could shoot, and he would pay me $25 per buck. He was very rich and he had a trucking company, I don't remember if it was Black, or Green or Brown, but the trucking company was some color. Well, I decided I had to make some money, so I started shooting deer. I sold him thirty deer that year. I know it was too many deer, but I had to get money somehow, and that is how I did it. Matter of fact, back then, everyone around here, they don't pay no attention to no law about deer. Everybody was hungry, it was the depression, and everybody kill deer all the time just for food. When you got some hungry kids at home, you ain't gonna worry about no game warden."

Another wildlife item that offers great food is the hog. There are two types of hogs in the wilds of South Texas. One is a domestic hog that has gone wild—a feral hog. The other is the Russian boar, imported into the state for sport, and called the razorback. These

should not be confused or taken for the javalin. These are not javalines. Further complicating the issue, there are now crosses of
the two hogs, providing a third type of hog. These hogs existed at
the turn of the last century, and provided an additional source of
food for the cowboy. My dad and Tío both told me that when cowboys were out working on horseback, and could not stop to kill and
butcher a hog, the hogs were roped, their tusks broken off with
stones, or a fencing tool, castrated, and turned loose for another
day. De-tusking hopefully eliminated the risk of being bitten and
maimed at some later confrontation, and the castration increases
weight, and reduces a gamey taste in the meat.

3

Life on the Rancho Las Blancas

Being Antonio Salinas's son, and living on his ranch, Juan always had the best of horses, equipment, and help. Juan rode as soon as he was old enough to stay on a horse. He learned to rope as soon as he had the strength to swing the loop. He had so many animals around him that his entire day consisted of practicing his riding and roping skills.

Juan was fortunate to have the best horseflesh around. Papá Antonio loved horses and always had none but the best. This was very important in helping Tío Juan become an expert calf roper—a calf roper without a good horse is just a roper. A roper with a good horse is potentially a champion calf roper. It was at this stage of his life that Tío Juan developed an eye for good mounts.

Tío Juan talked about being on horseback while he worked cattle from the time he was about eight years old until the time he was eighty-five years old. He talked about working cattle the old way when he was a boy. That meant gathering all the cattle and circling them with men on horses and holding them at bay, and working each head, one by one. Working meant branding, ear notching, doctoring, or simply separating an animal that was ready for market.

After encircling a large number of cattle, young Juan rode into the bunch with his horse and rope, to rope whichever animal the ground crew wanted. As I talked to Tío Juan one evening when he was ninety-two years old, he spoke with longing and sentiment about the hundreds of calves he went in and got with his rope. He roped the calf and dragged it out to the cowboys on foot. He quoted one of his old cowboy mentors, "*Tú los lazas, y yo los barbeo*" ("You rope 'em and I'll dog them [wrestle them to the ground]"). Juan rode his horse into the herd slowly, picked out the calf or heifer that needed roping, roped the animal, dallied the rope around his saddle horn, and pulled or dragged the animal out to the cowboys working afoot, on the ground. Once the animal was among the cowboys, one either grabbed the animal by a front leg and flank; picked up the animal slightly and dropped it to the ground; or grabbed the animal by the jaw, twisted it quickly to one side, causing the animal to fall to the ground for the necessary work—branding, castration, or doctoring, the latter being *barbeando,* or dogging to the ground. This was a necessity, as the cattle were too far from the hacienda to utilize the *corrales de leña*: there were no squeeze chutes at the time, there were no pick-up trucks either, and there were no freeze brands. The animals had to be dragged out to the burning fires for branding.

Tío Juan related that in the early 1900s, from oral history passed to him, the Hacienda Las Blancas was very similar to a hacienda of the 1800s established by the Spaniards. The passage of time brought little change from the ranches of old. There was still very little barbed wire, there was no electricity, and there was no indoor plumbing and no running water. The techniques and technology used on the ranch were the same. Tío Juan told me that they survived on beef, goats, chickens, guineas and their eggs, milk from cows and goats, butter from the same, and cheese from these. Flour and beans came from Laredo. My mother, Mamá Mucia, talked about inviting a sharecropper in for a meal, and after he ate the main course, he sat and talked to them while he helped himself to spoonful after spoonful of butter—apparently a rare item for him.

While the cowboys and their families usually had plenty to eat on the ranch, every roundup one or two head were slaughtered to provide beef for the families. The way it usually went was that toward the end of the roundup one of the old cowboys would insist that one or two steers had gone into shock, *ese becerro se acalambró* (that calf has gone into shock), and once going into shock was going to die, and therefore should be slaughtered for beef. It was a game of sorts, an excuse to dedicate two or three head of beef to provide food for the ranch families.

Life in the Becerra region was typical for the times. There was no electricity, and no running water, and no indoor plumbing. Water came from creeks, water wells, and the rain barrel. Catching water from rain gutters was very common. Typically, a 55-gallon drum stood at an outside corner close to the kitchen. The rain gutters drained into this barrel. A piece of burlap cloth covered the barrel top to keep out impurities, and nearby hung a dipper on a piece of string or wire. Whoever desired a drink walked up uncovered the barrel and used the dipper to get a drink. Water for cooking came from this barrel.

La Becerra was somewhat better off than most small communities were—it had a barber, and a visiting pharmacist. The pharmacist who came from Encinal, a Mr. Guerrero, father of Johnny Guerrero who worked at the Central Drug Store in Laredo for many years, would act as the unofficial physician and prescribe what he thought was appropriate. The pharmacist and a Catholic priest visited about once a month. There were about thirty families scattered at the various pastures surrounding the main ranches, and the population was about one hundred. The Las Blancas was right at 14,000 acres, but the acreage covered by the population represented at La Becerra was about fifty thousand acres.

There was a small school and most of the children went there for years. The Salinas children attended either there or the Salinas Ranch school near Encinal until they were teenagers, then they attended school in Laredo. In time, all of the children took on their own personality, character, and occupation. Juan became the cattle rancher. Anything that meant horses and cows, and other farm animals found Juan in the very middle. Jose Maria, nicknamed Chema, took an interest in farming and planting. Although there was no abundance of water, Chema found a way to grow hay and the contemporary crops from the sandy soil. During these years, the young men were in the learning stages, learning from the hired help that had been in these occupations for decades. Mucia, my mom, was the tall, gangly, quiet one. She read books and studied. She later would attribute her detached retinas and poor eyesight to the kerosene lanterns used for reading. Margarita, or Maggie, was the roly-poly, happy-go-lucky one in the bunch. She mostly followed Mucia's example, but got more involved in the household duties. Antonio, or Tony, being the youngest, played around, in wonder at the adults around him. He was ten years younger than Juan. Momma told a story about the kids running around playing tag one afternoon. Tony was then five years of age, and he suddenly stopped his chase, and came to Mamá Minnie asking for breast milk. "*Mamá, quiero teta,*" Tony asked between gasps. She gladly complied with his request. He suckled for a couple of minutes, then stopped and ran off to continue the game. Tony would later join Juan in the ranching duties, and follow him into the rodeo arena.

Tío Juan took to cowboying in earnest, running and working cattle the same as the early ranchers had one hundred years before him. Juan used the same techniques and equipment they used. Juan did not see and use a sisal rope until he was twenty years old. All earlier ropes were *riatas,* made from interwoven leather strips. Cattle grazed on native grasses. Men and animals suffered the brutal South Texas heat, and when grass was scarce, the Tejano cowboys had devised a method of alternative feeding, that of burning the thorns off prickly pear cactus. As mentioned, in Spanish the process is called *chamuscando* (singeing). The pear burner was not available yet so the cowboys gathered dry mesquite wood, piled it aside a pear bush, and lit the fire. They repeated the process on every large pear bush they saw, or they brought large chunks of cactus on pitchforks, held it over the fire to burn off the thorns, until they had enough cactus to feed the herd. Tío said that this was an extremely hot job. Sometimes the heat was so intense it blistered hands, chest, forehead, and thighs. The rough cowboys refused to back off until the cactus was ready.

"I know of a couple of young cowboys who damaged their eyes permanently from working too close to the burning fires," Tío Juan told me one day. I have often wondered if the macular degeneration he suffered in his eighties and nineties might not have started way back when he burned pear the old way. Tío Juan had great faith in burning pear as a supplement for feeding the herd. He preferred it to baled hay or grass. He told me a story, which I think was the beginning of his undying faith in the benefits of burning pear: "I had these two pastures and about fifty head of cattle in each one of them. One of the pastures had water from a water well, and the other had a stock earthen tank that filled only if it rained. One thing led to another, and suddenly we were in the middle of a drought that lasted about a year and a half. The earthen tank went dry, and I had no place to put the fifty head of cows. The market price was almost nothing, so I did not want to sell them. So, we started burning pear. We burned pear for those cattle for a whole year and some months. We did not burn pear for any other pasture. When the drought broke, I compared the two herds of cows, the burned pear pasture cows were in much better condition than the others were, and they had not had any water in a whole year and some."

In the springtime, right about Lent and Easter, the cactus plant will produce new leaves. The new tender leaves have thick stubble instead of fine, thin, sharp needles. The stubble can still hurt, because it is the beginning of what will become thorns. Since time immemorial, Tejanos have taken these tender new leaves, shaved or cut the thorns, the stubble, and created a magnificent dish. It is a delicacy to some, and the dish is called nopalitos, literally little cactus. After de-thorning with a knife, cut the nopalitos into small squares or long strips about half an inch wide, then boil thoroughly. After boiling, the nopalitos are ready to prepare into a variety of dishes. Most popular are: fried with eggs, or fried with chorizo and eggs, fried with red chile and shrimp. Any way you fix them the dish is very popular. It is usually a Lenten dish, usually served with refried beans and tortillas.

Tío shared a joke with me about nopalitos. He said it was a true story. "I walked into this restaurant, and they had nopalitos as the blue-plate special of the day. Trying to be funny I asked the waitress how much it cost for the *chamusque*, for the burned pear, and she came right back at me and said 'three dollars per steer.' Everybody laughed; I shut up and ordered nopalitos."

By far the most active days of the year at the La Becerra community were those nearest to the Día de San Juan, formerly celebrated widely in Mexico and South Texas. It became a big holiday at La Becerra. Tío Juan told me that it was usually a three-day affair. People came from the nearby ranches and camped out in the ample space. People showed up from Encinal, Laredo, and the smaller towns ready to join in the festivities. There were horse races, calf roping, dances, a huge *carne asada,* and other festivities.

Tío Juan told me that on one Día de San Juan, in 1915, the Guerra family brought out a beautiful horse named Hindenburg. It was a racehorse, and word was that the Guerras wanted to sell the horse. On the second day of the fiesta, the men prepared for several horse races. A Mr. Marroquin from Laredo came to La Becerra, and he was there to see Hindenburg, and possibly make an offer to buy the horse.

It was arranged that before any of the races, Hindenburg would be run down the straight quarter-mile track, so that Mr. Marroquin could time the horse with a stopwatch. A pistol shot at the starting gate would mark the start of the run, giving Mr. Marroquin the opportunity to start his stopwatch. The horse would run in the direction of the finish line where Mr. Marroquin would stop the watch as the horse crossed the finish line some two thousand feet away.

The shot rang out, Mr. Marroquin pressed on the head of the stopwatch with his thumb, and looked down the track as the beautiful horse sped toward the finish line. As the seconds ticked away, Mr. Marroquin kept looking back and forth at the horse, then at the stopwatch, amazed at the horse's speed. After several seconds, before Mr. Marroquin could look up the horse was upon him, ran him over, and Mr. Marroquin died instantly. He was loaded in the back of a one-horse buggy express and taken to Laredo for burial.

Life on the Las Blancas continued until the early 1920s. Tío Juan told me that he pushed cattle for sale into Laredo, cross-country. Contrary to my belief, Juan said that at the turn of the century and for several years thereafter, there were no fences on most of the ranches in the South Texas area. Nobody fenced off the pastures. When you rounded up, you worked everybody's cattle. If you had a neighbor's cattle in your bunch, you would pen them and advise the neighbor. He said that often he received word that he had cattle on someone else's land near Laredo, or near Encinal, and he would take two or three cowboys on horseback to retrieve the animals.

The cattle drive to Laredo took three days. At night everyone would camp out in the open. They took food and bedrolls to bed down for the night. Juan said the final night was spent at the north edge of Laredo at a little goat ranch owned by a woman by the name of Rodriguez, whom everyone called La Docha. Her little ranch was near what today we would describe as Del Mar Boulevard and McPherson Avenue in Laredo, Texas. The following day they would drive the herd all the way into the meat packing plant and cattle pens that were located near downtown Laredo.

In talking about the three-day trip into Laredo, I heard an interesting story: "We was coming up on a lake about 10 miles away. I sent a cowboy up on ahead to check and see if the approach to the lake was open. He rode off and we kept pushing the cattle toward Laredo. Several hours later, the cowboy come up to where we was. He said that the water was there for cattle, and the way was open, but the woman that owned the land, she said she would let the cattle in unless Juan Salinas came to her ranch and paid her a visit and bedded her. That put me into some kind of a bind."

I then asked him about the outcome: "well did you have to go meet her and bed her?"

"We got the cattle to water," was the only response.

"But, tell me about the woman who she was, and what happened, what you had to do to get the cattle to water."

"We got the cattle to water," is the only response I got.

On one of our Sunday drives, we were at the north end of a pasture known as Las Conchas. There are hundreds of huge prehistoric oyster shells in the area. Spanish for shell is *concha*, hence Las Conchas. The north end of the pasture is the highest point in the area. Tío explained the geography: "I can't see too well no more, but if you look south-southwest, you will see a landmark. That landmark is a little mountain, a mesa actually. It has a flat top. The Spaniards named that landmark. They named it *Cerrito Prieto*, Dark Little

Mountain. The ranch is named Cerrito Prieto. I been there. The peoples that own it have parties every once in a while, and we go there. There is a huge house at the base of the Cerrito. It feels funny in the afternoons, when you can look north, south, and east and see the hot bright sun, but by that time, the sun is behind the Cerrito, and the whole ranch area is in the shade of the Cerrito.

"The Spaniards named other landmarks in the area. I usually only relied on the Cerrito Prieto to get my bearings. Just get up on a hill and look around for it, and you knew where you were. Due west of Encinal, and also south-southwest of Encinal are the tall hills called the *Piloncillo* (a cone of brown sugar), and then farther south from there is another monument, two hills side by side called *Las Dos Hermanas* (the Two Sisters). I don't see these hills too much, 'cause I almost never ride out that way. Same for the big and very long range of hills, as you travel east of Encinal, and almost when you get to Freer, Texas, you hit like a long line of hills. The Spaniards called it the *escarpamiento* (the escarpment), and they say lots of peoples used it to get their bearings. The hills go for many, many miles, just a long row of hills."

Tío Juan told me that the first time he rode from La Becerra to Laredo he noticed that the creek water flow appeared strange to him. Juan was born and raised near the La Becerra Creek that is a part of the Nueces River watershed, and the water flows to the north or northeast. As one approaches Laredo from La Becerra, all the creeks flow into the Rio Grande watershed; thus, the water flows south or southwest. To a Becerreño, this was strange.

"There is one other landmark we use when we taking cattle cross-country from Las Blancas into Laredo. If you come to a high spot, a hill or bluff and look southwest, you can see the blue outline of the mountains in Mexico. From Las Blancas it was a straight shot to Laredo if you traveled toward the highest peak. On a clear day, you can see these mountains as you drive to Laredo on IH 35. Wait till you come to the last hills on the way in about the 9-mile marker then look south-southwest, and there they are. If you aren't looking for them, you might miss them 'cause they is just a real light blue outline."

I asked Tío Juan about eating and cooking while they rode into Laredo, or while they worked away from the home ranch. "Well we always gotta take food. Even if we just working for one day. If we could come back, we come back to the house or to camp to eat. If we set up a camp we coming back to, I usually left one fellow behind to fix the meals. When we had canned goods, we usually depend on them a lot. We always gotta cook a big pot of beans, and a huge basket of flour tortillas. If we had fresh meat, we cook that too. Usually on short trips, it was just tortillas and beans.

"Even when we go to Laredo to leave cattle, we take a pot for the beans and a sack of flour, and lots of *carne seca*. We stop along the way at a lake or tank, or a creek holding water, and we use that water for cooking and drinking. We fill up our canteens. We used to drink water wherever we found it. As long as it was not stagnant, we used it. It was rainwater, and if it was clean, it worked. It would take us three days to get to Laredo, so we stopped and cooked pinto beans with salt pork, and cooked tortillas.

"If we had jerky, we would shred it and make a soup we call *caldillo*. You just rehydrate the venison, add salt, pepper, garlic, onion, a potato if you have one, and make a real delicious soup. You gotta remember that by the time you sit down to eat you been working five, six, or more hours, you get plenty hungry and we not too picky about what we eat. When you hungry like that out in the *monte*, everything tastes great.

"We never worry about no game warden. If we out working for several days, when we got hungry we kill a doe, and we eat fresh meat, and make carne seca out of what was left over. If you have five to ten men, it don't take long to eat a doe or a buck. Usually the meat don't have time to spoil. But if we got some meat left over, or if we kill a head of beef, one of the cowboys would make carne seca. Making carne seca was an art, you don't see too many peoples now a days that can make carne seca the old way. It takes lots of time and patience, and a knife and a sharpening stone. You need the stone, because making carne seca takes a real sharp knife. From a piece of meat, usually a big muscle, say 4 inches around and maybe 6 to 10 inches long, one starts to unravel or unroll the muscle with a sharp knife, little by little cut and unroll or unravel, until the big muscle is extended into a small sheet of very thin meat, say 2 or 3 feet square. You do this to as much meat as you have and you might end up with 6 or 8 square feet of meat. In Spanish, you say you *acecinar la carne* (dry the meat).

"The meat is then salted and put out to dry. If we working cattle, we hang it on a barb wire fence close to the house, or close to the camp. If not, then just hang it on a mesquite bush. The meat is left to dry all day long, then taken in at night, so the dew don't gets it wet again. Finally, after a few days, the meat is completely dry and ready to eat. It sure is good. You don't get to eat old style jerky anymore. This stuff they sell in the stores, that may be dried meat, but it ain't no jerky, and it tastes like salted cardboard. Venison jerky made the old way has a very special good taste.

"If we be working for several days or weeks, then we gotta plan the food. We usually take a wagon, with boxes full of tin dishes and cups, pots and pans, and food of course. But, the food, it don't change much; its beans, rice, tortillas, and sometimes meat, and always plenty of coffee. When we have a big camp, we always make *panochas*. I know, I know, nobody likes to call them panochas anymore, because panocha means vagina, but pussy also means cat, and we still say pussycat. Panocha means vagina, but it also means camp bread, *pan de campo*, and some people prefer to call it *pan de campo*, but I always call it *panocha*. Panochas are made in a dutch oven, and when we on a long *campo*, we usually carry two or three dutch ovens, so the cook can makes several panochas for every meal. The panocha is made out of flour just like a big biscuit, and placed in the greased iron pan, which is placed on burning coals, and covered with an iron lid that has a short edge or brim on it, and then the cook fills the lid with burning coals. Them cooks they know when the bread is cooked and they take the lid off, the bread is ready, and they just take it out, put the bread in a big basket lined with a cloth, and just keep adding bread as it comes out. When the cowboys serve their plate, they just reach in the breadbasket and break off a piece of bread to eat with their meal. After we eat, we sometimes break off another piece of panocha, and pour molasses on it for dessert. If we don't got no molasses, we use *sirope del cone-jito* (Brer Rabbit syrup), or *sirope de la casita* (Log Cabin brand), a syrup that used to come in a little tin can looked like a little cabin."

On one of our Saturday morning rounds in 1990, we went to check the three windmills on the Martineña Road east of Encinal. It was early March, and the weather was beautiful, about 65 degrees, clear sky, and no wind, just beautiful. Looking at the countryside, the Spanish dagger, the *pita* in Spanish, were in bloom. White plumes about 2 feet high come out of the center of the spine nests, the sharp blades of the tree. I commented on the beauty to Tío. He responded, "yeah, those are real purty. Something you probably don't known, 'cause you never was in no poor condition, and in no depression, is that we used to eat them white flowers. Yeah, we picked them and got a big tub full, and the womens at home they cooked the white petals in oil or *manteca de puerco* (lard), added *chile, tomate y cebolla* (pepper, tomato, and onion), and cooked them just like a big pot of *arroz*, rice. It tastes pretty good."

As we drove on, a whirlwind, or dust devil, a *remolino*, picked up about 20 yards ahead of us, then met the pick-up and shook us as we drove through it. Tío crossed thumbs and index finger of both hands and let out a chant. "What did you say, and why?" I asked.

"I said '*Cruz, cruz que vaya el diablo y venga Jesús*' ('Cross, cross, may the devil go and Jesus comes'). The old folks, they say that the dust devil is the devil himself, so to protect us from the devil, we cross our fingers on both hands, and say that little prayer, and we are safe."

Tío mentioned to me that when they were working away from the main ranch, they used black ropes to surround the camp at night. They laid the rope out in a circle around the bedrolls and campfire. He said that rattlesnakes are afraid of blue indigo snakes, also called black snakes, because the blue indigo snake will eat a rattlesnake. Tío said he saw blue indigos eat rattlesnakes on several occasions. Although none of the men ever got a snake bite in camp, Tío said he was with three cowboys when rattlesnakes bit them. Of the three, two survived and one died. Tío said that the area of the snakebite swelled up to four times normal, and the men got a

very high fever. He told me that there was always one cowboy in
the group that knew the *rezo de la vibora*, the prayer of the snake.
In actuality, the prayer of the snake consisted of the first five verses
from the book of John in the Bible. They prayed these verses by
the bedside of the victim. Tío said he never learned it, but that it
was quite a long prayer. He said they prayed it repeatedly.

> 1. In the beginning was the Word
> The Word was with God
> And the Word was God.
> 2. He was with God in the beginning.
> 3. Through him all things came into being,
> Not one thing came into being except through him.
> 4. What has come into being in him was life,
> Life that was the light of men;
> 5. And light shines in darkness,
> And darkness could not overpower it.

One evening we sat in the den talking and watching television
and he told me to look in a drawer in one of the end tables. The
drawer was full with several hundred rattles from rattlesnakes. "I
kill rattlesnakes all my life, and I just decided to start saving the
rattles, and put 'em in this drawer, and just kept collecting and
kept collecting.

"Lots of peoples get all scared with a rattlesnake, but I just walk
up to them, with a short stick about 3 feet long, and start to whack
'em little by little on the head, until I knock 'em out, then I walk up
and step on the head with my boot heel, take out my knife and cut
off the head, then cut off the rattle.

"One of the things I loved to do is joke with the cowboys with
a dead snake. I walk up, and hit it with the stick, then when it is
dead, and before the cowboy can see me cut the head off, I quickly
cut the head off, then pick up the snake and throw it at the cowboy,
and hit him in the chest with the fully extended rattlesnake. Ha,
ha, ha, ha, I seen so many cowboys yell, cry, and jump and run,
when the snake hit them. Ha, ha ha ha, I sure had lots of fun with
them dead snakes."

Sometimes, on their cattle drive visits to Laredo if Juan and Tony did not want to disturb the elderly Tía Chente, they stayed at the jail. Being that Papá Antonio was the Webb County sheriff, they were more than welcome. They stabled their horses there, and slept in one of the unoccupied cells. Tío Juan said he remembered vividly that there was a gallows in the back yard of the jail. Once in Laredo, Juan stayed for a two or three day visit. He visited his tías Inocente and Margarita and sometimes stayed at their house. After he finished with business and some social life, he left early in the morning and was back at Las Blancas by evening, a much speedier one-day trip, unhampered by the herd of cattle.

4

The Move to Encinal

In the early 1900s the Martin family, related by blood to the Salinases, did not have any adult males to manage their financial affairs and businesses. They relied heavily on their cousin Antonio Salinas, my grandfather (Papá Antonio), to administer their businesses. One of the last tasks assigned to Antonio was to buy ranches for the several branches of the young family. He was to buy a ranch large enough to provide each child with five to ten thousand acres. Papá Antonio was able to find large tracts of land from what we know today as Artesia Wells, Texas, 12 miles north of Encinal, all the way to the Martineña Ranch headquarters 5 miles southeast of Encinal. The acreage he found for purchase was enough to provide each of the ten branches 11,000 acres. The name of the huge spread was La Martineña Ranch. Each of the spreads either had or acquired its own name: La Bonita (the pretty one, feminine), El Willy (obviously for a man or boy named Willy), El Colorado (the red, masculine), Las Abras (the valleys), La Magueyoza (maguey being a century plant, magueyoza indicating a large amount of maguey plant; the maguey is the plant used for making tequila in Mexico); the Magueyoza was later changed to La Retamosa (filled with Retama trees), El Jardín (the garden), Los Olmos (the elms), El Tecolote (the owl), Las Comas (the wild persimmon), and La Martineña (simply a group or gathering of martins), sometimes called La Hacienda.

As he purchased all of this ranch land for his cousins, Antonio decided to buy acreage near Encinal for himself. He sold his holdings, the Las Blancas Ranch in East Webb County at La Becerra, and bought 15,000 acres of land just south of Encinal. Already in failing health, he wanted Mamá Minnie and their children to be closer to civilization, closer to Laredo, and closer to a main thoroughfare. He found land that had belonged to Webb County's Judge J. M. Rodriguez, 3 miles south of Encinal, on a main highway, then U.S. 81, later to become IH 35. Papá Antonio died in 1923, two years after buying the new ranch.

On one of our evening chats that became characteristic of our several-year relationship, Tío Juan asked me to go to the hat tree and retrieve a small wooden item.

"Get that little piece of wood. It is a whip handle. I want to give it to you."

He looked at it carefully, examined all four sides of the square part, and having confirmed what he knew already gave me the piece of wood. The whip handle is a piece of native ebony wood about 14 inches long. Although it looks like a whip handle it is obviously a museum piece—viewed but never used. The piece is about a half-inch round and square. It is hand carved beautifully, albeit primitively.

"One of the cowboys carved that for my Daddy out of a piece of ebano, ebony from right here on the ranch, and gave it to him," Tío related.

The round/oval part is smooth, and is about 4 inches long. The square part is about 10 inches long, and each side has artwork on it.

One side says, "*Cirbo a mi dueno Antonio Salinas*" (I serve my master, Antonio Salinas). At the top of the carving are what appear to be a thistle flower and the image of an angel.

Another side displays a long vine and leaves.

Another side reads, "*Febrero Biernes Fecha 2 01 de 1909*" (February Friday 2 01, of 1909.)

The final side displays another type of vine with flowers.

It is such a beautiful and priceless piece, I keep it stored in my safe. You can sense immediately that it is something special. I lost it once for about five years, and lost sleep over the loss. Then when we moved to Rancho Santana, I found it stuffed in a toy basket.

One of the children, or one of the cleaning girls thought it was a toy and put it with the others.

At the Santana, Papá Antonio built a large, 2,000-square-foot wooden Victorian-type home with surrounding south side and east side porches. He also built a mother-in-law house, north of the big house, for my great-grandmother, Margaret Riley. Margaret's son, Zack Light, also worked on the ranch and had quarters elsewhere. By this time, great-grandmother Margaret Riley was Granny; Zack Light Jr. was Tío Isaac, or Tío Zack.

Juan led the huge logistical move to the Encinal ranch. It took several cross-country trips from Las Blancas to the new ranch—Santana Ranch. Tío Juan told me that the first time he came to the new ranch he drove all the cattle, mules, donkeys, and other smaller stock together with about ten horsemen, and that when he got to the Jaboncillo (china berry) Creek about a half mile from where the main ranch is, it was running full to its banks. Juan and all the rest of the men and animals forded the full creek.

I questioned Tío Juan on the geography of the area in the 1920s. I wanted to confirm or disaffirm a historical fact I had heard earlier. Tío confirmed that at the turn of the century the geography of northern and central Webb County consisted of grassy plains, with brush and tall trees confined to the wooded creek beds, *ramaderos*. Tío agreed with the theory that the infestation and proliferation of mesquite brush and trees came from seeds brought to Texas in Mexican cattle and deposited on Texas soil in cattle droppings; he also added that before Mexican cattle there were frequent grass fires that kept brush under control.

In the 1990s I exchanged a letter with my distant cousin J. C. Martin Jr., who had been in bad health. I thought a letter might cheer him up. He responded in a couple of weeks, reminiscing about family history, and explained that Papá Antonio had established the Martin ranches around Encinal. He stated that in those days popular thought was that creek beds, ramaderos, were more valuable than grassy plains. Today ranchers spend thousands of dollars trying to establish grassy plains, defoliating the brush and cactus.

The Salinases became good neighbors to most who lived in Encinal. Most new workers and sharecroppers were from Encinal. To neighbors, Mamá Minnie was Doña Minerva, although her name was not Minerva, but simply Minnie. As young Tony grew up he became very popular, definitely the extrovert of the family. He enjoyed fiestas, dances, and playing pool. By his early teenage years, Tony had developed into a tremendous athlete. As an adult, he was tall at 6 feet 1 or 2, and thin and muscular and weighed in at about 200 pounds. He was an excellent football player when he attended Laredo High School, and later excelled in his brief stay at St. Louis High School, in San Antonio, later to change its name to St. Mary's.

This athletic prowess crossed over to the roping arena. When Tony became of age, he proved to be better and faster than Juan was—an excellent calf roper. Most of the time however, Juan, the older, slower, but more consistent roper, won the matches, but Tony won his share.

Mamá Mucia and Maggie spent more and more of their time in Laredo, it being more accessible after the move to Encinal. In addition, they were in high school and became involved in the activities that dominate those years. Chema, in the meantime, cleared more and more land, and drilled water wells for irrigation purposes. He made tanks, laid pipelines, and generally pursued the farming occupation. He grew hay, onions, and other crops that grew in the area. Tony and Juan continued as cowboys, honing the skills that, unbeknownst to them, would take them in the near future to the rodeo championship competitions of the world.

Granny, Margaret Riley, helped around the house. She was the old mother hen, helping her daughter Minnie and her five young children. Zack Light was a *caporal*, foreman, leading workers in their daily chores. Although all men of the era knew how to work cattle and work at roundups, Zack showed a preference for the farming side of the equation, and was always helping his nephew Chema get in the crops and tend to the fields.

Juan and to a lesser degree Tony, who was still a boy, rode and worked all over north Webb County, wherever Salinas cattle might

Four generations on the Salinas Ranch, 1937. Seated, Margaret
Riley ('Granny'). Left to right: Abe Palacios Jr., Mucia
Salinas Palacios, Minnie Light Salinas ('Grandma')

roam. Barbed wire fences were still a novelty and not found often.
From the time he was old enough to ask his father to let him drop
out of school to work the ranches permanently, to the time he died,
Juan loved the ranch, cattle, horses, and the rough terrain that we
know as the South Texas Brush Country.

Juan said he was riding his horse about 10 miles south of Encinal one day when he spotted a Model T Ford approaching. In
the car were two men. As it got closer, he noticed it was Sam Jordan from Encinal driving the car, with another man. As they met,
Mr. Jordan asked Juan to dismount: "Juan, get down, I want you
to meet someone." Juan dismounted, and Mr. Jordan introduced
him: "Juan, this is Mr. Joe Finley, he comes from the Midwest, and
he has come to manage the Callaghan Ranch." The two men shook
hands.

The Callaghan Ranch is officially the Callaghan Land and Pas-
toral Company, 12 miles south of Encinal, just off U.S. 81, which
is now I 35. It consisted of more than 100,000 acres. Again, Juan
reminded me that there were no fences separating ranches at the

time. After Mr. Finley took over, Juan said, the fences started going up, and shortly they knew that the Callaghan was running sheep. We know now that eventually Mr. Joe Finley worked hard, and managed to buy the Callaghan Ranch, which today operates under the leadership of my good friends, Joe B. Finley Jr., his wife Mary, and his daughters Alicia, Ana Maria, Amanda, Amy, and Mary Jo. The ranch has shrunk some but continues as one of the largest working cattle ranches in the world.

Through the years, the South Texas ranch owners have tried whatever they could to undertake whatever ventures were available to make money. The idea is to sell your product and make a profit. It has not been easy. The Callaghan Ranch at the turn of the century was trying something new, sheep. I don't know the details or the particulars, but I don't think that sheep worked. Eventually all landowners started fencing their land. It was bound to happen; you just could not have all these separate ranches adjacent to each other with no fences. Sheep precipitated it, but it had to happen, and it did.

After sheep, it was horses, all landowners trying to make a buck raised horses to sell to the government, to sell to whoever wanted horses. It came and went, and did not work. Again, landowners settled on cattle. It has always been very hard to make money on cattle in the South Texas Brush Country, but landowners keep on trying. A good friend from Encinal has said that the government, with subsidies and mortgage moratoriums during the depression, has misled us all into thinking that the cattle business is a viable business in this country, when it actually is not, and is something we keep kidding ourselves about. Eight years out of ten we have a drought, cannot raise a decent calf crop, and we make barely enough to pay the bank note, which most of us have. Nevertheless, some of us keep doing it, we keep trying—it's in our blood. Some ranchers are very fortunate in that they have oil or gas royalties to help pay the bills. These ranches are profitable, but if it were not for the oil and gas revenue, profit would be questionable.

Mr. Joe Finley Sr. built an office at the Callaghan out of what used to be the ranch general store. At the entrance, in wrought iron, surrounded by a lariat loop, are found the following lines, which have always captured my attention:

> If you think you are beat, you are!
> If you think you dare not, you don't!
> If you would like to win, but think you can't!
> It's almost a cinch you won't!

Tío explained the struggle. "Most of the time it is very dry around here. Many times in my life, we have had two and three year periods without any rain. Many times a year and year and a half we get no rain. Twice in my lifetime, we had periods of five to seven years of no rain—not one drop. Nowadays I supplement feed by giving the cattle cottonseed cake, *mascarrote*. Or, we buy hay and give them hay, or we burn pear, *chamuscamos*. But when we first started here in the twenties, we had one seven-year drought, and we didn't have any money to feed them, I mean the cows were *como el caballo del gachupín, ya mero aprendía a no comer, cuando de repente se murió* (like the Spaniard's horse who almost learned to go without eating, and suddenly he died).

"After World War II, we had cattle all over the country. People thought the war was going to go on for more years, and everybody was producing lots and lots of cattle for the soldiers. Well, suddenly the war ended, and the market went down to almost nothing, about five cents a pound on the hoof. The government came in to take care of the problem. They sent field agents to visit all ranches. They come to me and they told me that they were going to kill 60 percent of my cows and pay me two dollars a head. They brought a big bulldozer, dug a huge grave, we pushed the cattle in with horses, then the government agents shot the cattle with .22 rifles. To me it was the most stupid and dumb thing I ever saw in my life. But, there was nothing I could do it was the American government. You take your two dollars a head, and go home and cry."

Throughout Tío Juan's life, he faced the demise of the cattle ranch. Slowly, ranches got smaller, operations changed. Ranch workers moved to the cities, small towns got smaller, some died completely. The cattle drives ended with the advent of cattle trucks and trains. Eventually, with a change of technology to diesel fuel, railroad switch towns were no longer necessary and disappeared soon thereafter. Tío Juan either did not notice this, or somehow worked around it. He always worked alongside his men. Moreover, he worked hard, long hours. Somehow, he was able to hang on longer than most, in getting and keeping good workers. Whatever the reason, he went well into the century working the ranch, and making it produce, notwithstanding the fact that the rest of the nation was witnessing the disappearance of fully integrated working cattle ranches. As I write I think of the four children I have in college today, five next year; I think that Tío's ability to make money at cattle ranching, and his ability to keep the money, was maybe because he had no children. Not to disparage his ability to work hard and make money, I just think that realistically he did not have that huge drain on the family income.

We all know that Tío Juan never spent more money than he had to. You can talk to any of the old cowboys in Encinal and they will tell you they never earned a living wage on the Salinas Ranch. I talked to Tío about wages once or twice.

"Used to be that we worked every day of the year—even Christmas and Easter. Cowboys earned $1.00 per day, and we worked from sunup to sundown. That was the wage. Every once in a while we would throw in flour, beans, venison. During roundups about twice a year, we killed a big steer, and everyone got fresh beef. Of course, we let the help kill all the deer, *javalin* (javelina), hog, and rabbits that they wanted.

"Then certain businesses started closing on Sunday. Pretty soon nobody worked on Sunday. Then several years later, certain businesses started closing at noon on Saturday. Then years later, nobody worked on Saturday either. Then the government jumped in and messed everything up with minimum wages. This didn't apply to us, 'cause it don't apply to ranches and farms, but the cowboys started going to other jobs where they got better money, and only had to work 8 hours a day. The government usually spoils everything anyway."

"How much were you paying your cowboys when I came to help you in 1987?" I asked.

"I was paying them $10 per day, plus room and board, but I still couldn't get too many to work for me. How much are you paying the guys that drive me around every day?"

"I am paying them $40 dollars a day, and we can only work them 8 or 9 hours each day." I answered.

"Forty dollars a day . . . you crazy. How can you give away such money? That is foolish. You are throwing money away."

I remember that at $10 per day we could only get drunks and vagabonds. At $40 per day, we did not do much better. Today it is almost impossible to find a cowboy who is willing to work and live on the ranch. The last cowboy I hired got $40 per day, and a nice air-conditioned two-bedroom cabin, all bills paid. He wasn't satisfied, and I wasn't satisfied. He wrecked the truck, burned out the tractor, and broke everything he touched. I haven't hired a permanent cowboy since. I just hire good cowboys for a day or two when I need them.

5

Young Juan Takes Over and the Roping Starts in Earnest

One of the reasons the family moved to the Encinal area was that Papá Antonio was in failing health. He suffered a cerebral stroke about 1918, and finally succumbed from its effects in 1923. The young family took the death extremely hard; their strength, their means of support was gone. In reversed roles, young J. C. Martin, and John Martin, known to the Salinases respectively as Tío Jose and Tío Juanito, served as executors of Papá Antonio's estate. Substantial debt required sale of half of the ranch. Mrs. Gertrude Chilton from Dallas, who already owned an equal amount on the east side of U.S. 81, a ranch known to this date as the San Román Ranch, purchased the acreage. With the Salinas purchase, the acreage doubled to about 15,000 acres. As I write, rumor on the street is that ownership will change soon for a reported $19 million.

By tacit agreement, Juan and Chema cared for Mamá Minnie, Juan running the cattle operation and Chema raising crops. The girls moved to Laredo to find work. Maggie found secretarial work in Laredo, and Mucia a job as a teacher, and they both lived with the tías Chente and Margarita.

Papá Antonio's last will and testament left everything to Mamá Minnie and their five children. However, Papá Antonio had been married before, his wife had died, and he had two sons from this previous marriage, Antonio the first, and Jose. Antonio and Jose became part of the second family; they got along very well. They saw each other as brothers in the second family, which they were. For some reason, Papá Antonio decided to leave them out of his

The Salinas brothers (Juan, l.; Tony, r.)

will. Jose and Antonio were jailers at the Webb County jail. Disappointed in being left out of the will, Jose and Antonio filed suit
to set aside Papá Antonio's will. After a few months of litigation,
Mamá Minnie's lawyers advised her to settle the lawsuit; otherwise, attorneys' fees would devour the estate value. Mamá Minnie
agreed, and the solution was to divide the ranch into eight equal
shares, Mamá Minnie getting her share at the home ranch, then

each of the children getting 948 acres. Antonio the first got Share One, Jose Share Two, Momma Mucia Share Three, Maggie Share Four, Juan Share Five, Tony Share Six, Chema Share Seven, and Mamá Minnie Share Eight.

After the settlement, Juan kept running Mamá Minnie's and his siblings' shares. The siblings had an opportunity to make their own money with their land if they wanted. For example, Momma Mucia, my mother, made an agreement with a sharecropper on a small portion of land. The sharecropper agreed to farm a small field, Momma would put up all the seed, and the mules and implements, and net proceeds would be distributed equally. Momma told me about going to visit the sharecropper on New Year's Day. The sharecropper lived in a tiny lean-to along a fence. Prickly pear cactus grew throughout the barbed wire fence. The sharecropper had cooked about two dozen *buñuelos,* a typical New Year's pastry, and not having a table, hung them on the prickly pear cactus for cooling. After they cooled, he took them down and kept them in an empty flour sack. A buñuelo is like a hot fried flour tortilla sprinkled generously with cinnamon and sugar.

With Papá Antonio gone, Juan had to obtain financing to get into the cattle business, and Tío Juanito Martin took him to meet the president of Laredo National Bank, Mr. Ben Alexander. Tío Juanito told him that Mr. Alexander knew the cattle business was a very insecure business and did not necessarily want to loan money on such a venture, "but don't worry. He'll probably jump about 3 feet off the floor when you tell him you need a loan for a cattle operation, and he'll hem and haw and disagree with you, but he will lend you the money."

It turned out exactly as Tío Juanito described. Juan met Mr. Alexander for the first time and he jumped and hollered and told Juan that a cattle ranch was the worst business in the world, and tried to discourage him, and asked him to get into another business, but when it was over, Mr. Alexander agreed to lend him the money. The relationship with Laredo National Bank continued until Juan's death in 1995. After Mr. Ben Alexander passed away, his son Maurice, a true cattleman and cowboy, continued as Juan's banker. Maurice felt the same way about the cattle business, knowing that it was a tough business, but being in the business, he felt obligated to help a colleague.

Juan never let the bank down; they enjoyed a good relationship for slightly over seventy years. If anything, Juan turned out to be an excellent businessman, and rarely needed to borrow money. After he established himself in the cattle-raising business, he bought his first automobile, a Model T Ford. He bought a new automobile every two years thereafter until autos started lasting more than two years. Once he started on the rodeo circuit, he bought a new car every year. He said he traded the car in and paid the balance of $300 to $350 every year. He often told me that he never bought a car on credit. His last auto was a 1993 Toyota pick-up, which he called La Coyota. He was ninety-two years of age. I wrote out the check for $16,000 that he signed and I delivered it to the dealer. He loved the little truck because it was easier for him to get in and out of, instead of a higher pick-up. To my knowledge, Tío Juan borrowed money three times in his life: first for beginning in business when Papá Antonio died; second to buy cattle, when he bought Share One of the Antonio Salinas Estate; and third when he built a new house at the Salinas Ranch in 1963. On each occasion, Juan paid back the money long before it was due.

After the first years of establishing the Santana Ranch, and years after Papá Antonio died, Juan began to venture out to Texas rodeos. These varied in sophistication and size. Some had all events, including bronc riding, bull riding, steer tripping, and bull dogging. Others were simply match ropings; a contest between two or more ropers, the winner of which would take the bet money; or a jackpot roping, where several ropers all contributed to a pot, winner take all. Travel for Tío Juan (and Tía Bertha, after they married in 1936) was always in a new Chevrolet automobile, pulling a two-horse shotgun trailer. Every year he attended the major rodeos in the state, including those in the Rio Grande Valley below Laredo, in Corpus Christi, San Antonio, Del Rio, Junction, San Angelo, Houston, Beaumont, Fort Worth, and Dallas, and points in between. Both Juan and Tony were popular in rodeo circles by 1930.

Fort Bend County Rodeo, Rosenberg, Texas, 1932.
Juan Salinas last row, second from right

American rodeo began in the 1800s, when they were simple contests between cowboys involving horses and cattle. By the early 1900s, the events were somewhat organized, but there was still no association or organization that established concrete rules and policy. This continued until 1936, the first year that Tío Juan went on the national rodeo circuit. Tío told me that a producer did not want to use the cowboy's entry fees as prize money, and offered very little prize money to produce a large rodeo in Boston. The producer stood to make a lot of money, yet was not willing to share with the cowboys. The cowboys formed what they called the Cowboys Turtle Association, and threatened to strike the rodeo in Boston if they were not treated fairly with the prize money (see charter and petition on pp. 86–87). After several days, the producer relented. The Cowboys Turtle Association was the first successful organization for rodeo cowboys. Before the Cowboys Turtle Association, a producer started what he called the World Championship Rodeo in New York City. It was a self-proclaimed world championship, as there was nobody establishing it as such. One or two other rodeos in the country also called themselves world championships, but the New York Championship Rodeo was considered the world championship, albeit unofficial, and rodeo historians and the rodeo fraternity recognize titles won there as such. Several years after formation of the Cowboys Turtle Association, after establishing rules and a plan, the Association changed its name to the Rodeo Cowboys Association (RCA). With a board of directors, dues-paying membership, rules and regulations, and the ability to sanction rodeos and come up with a championship plan, the RCA created an official World Championship Rodeo, what we know today as the National Finals Rodeo. At first the finals rodeo was held in Oklahoma City, but later moved to Las Vegas where it is held in December of each year. In 1975, the RCA changed its name to the Professional Rodeo Cowboys Association (PRCA). Tío Juan was a member of the Cowboys Turtle Association and of the Rodeo Cowboys Association as an active member, and later as a lifetime member became a member of the PRCA. I have a photo of Tío Juan and Tía Bertha at a Cowboys Turtle Association banquet at the Texas Hotel in Fort Worth in 1940.

Having Tía Bertha with him provided much-appreciated companionship, and unbeknownst to him, a family historian. Tía probably knew what she was doing in collecting all the photos and other memorabilia from rodeo to rodeo through the years. I am sure she knew that someday, someone would enjoy them and share them with others.

One of my treasured possessions is Tío Juan's gold membership card in the Rodeo Cowboys Association. It is card number 1592, it is a metal card, it certifies that Juan Salinas is a lifetime member, and is signed by Chas. Colbert, Secretary.

Other smaller rodeos and match ropings kept Juan and Tony active almost every weekend of the year. Juan told me of attending a huge roping in Falfurrias, Texas, in the early 1930s. By that time, he was a card-carrying professional. After he and Tony paid their entry fees, the other ropers mounted a protest and tried to get them disqualified before the roping started. Their point was that professionals should not be able to compete against amateurs.

Mr. Ed Rachal, a Falfurrias businessman, ended the argument when he told the protesters that they had to let the Salinases rope because they had not advertised it as an amateur rodeo. They had advertised it as a jackpot roping, with ropers paying a cash entry fee, and the winners taking a large portion of the entry fees—professional in every sense of the word. The rub was that only Juan and Tony were card-carrying professionals. Juan won first place and Tony second.

They also roped in Laredo, and in Cotulla, Alice, Corpus Christi, Uvalde, San Angelo, Carrizo Springs, San Antonio, Shiner, Halletsville, and every small town around that promoted a rodeo or roping.

After the move to Santana Ranch, Juan became more active in calf roping in area match ropings. They are matches, because the event is actually a competition between two ropers, or a team of ropers versus another team. By agreement, it can be a six-calf match, or eight-calf match; he also spoke of many twenty-calf matches. It is a timed event. Whichever roper ropes all calves faster, or in less time, wins the match. This entitles the winner to the bet money, made in advance of the roping. Mostly Juan was successful. It would be several years before he launched into statewide and nationwide competition.

Lee Karr, the cowboy and photographer from Kerrville, described an early match roping in Sonora, Texas. It was 1935 and Lee was working as a young cowboy on a nearby ranch. He could not attend, could not get off work. Juan Salinas was matched against Ted Powers, a champion roper from the vicinity. It was a twenty-calf match. Lee says that the Sonora fairgrounds and arena swelled to four times its normal attendance, the largest attendance ever, up to that time. Juan Salinas did not miss a loop that afternoon, and won the match handily.

Tío told me about one of their trips back from a Falfurrias roping. "My brother Tony and I was driving back from a roping in Falfurrias, and we was driving through the little town of San Diego, Texas. This was before Tony got married. Right on the southeast side of the town, the big San Diego Creek crosses the town, and before a bridge was a white building on the edge of the creek, and it was a cantina, and we decided to stop and get a hamburger and a couple of beers.

"We walked in, and there was a young man there with a real pretty girl. We sat down at a table, and the bartender recognized us and started making a big *borlote*, hullabaloo, about the Salinas brothers, and the roping champions, and so on, and he told the young man and the young woman who we were. She seemed a little impressed, the man didn't seem to care one way or another.

"Well we ordered and we was sitting there waiting for our order, when Tony decides he wants to start talking to the pretty girl, and she apparently wants to talk to Tony. You can tell that this is bothering the young man, but the girl she don't mind, so Tony he don't mind either. Before long, Tony tells the girl to move on over to our table, and she gets up to move over, and the young man he blows up.

"'What the hell do you think you are doing?' he yelled. Tony was very calm, and he said that the young girl was coming to sit with us on her own, and if he did not like it, it was too bad. Well the young man started cussing, and saying that the Salinases were a bunch of this and that and the other, and we just kind of laughed at him. The young man left, yelling, and said he was going to go get the sheriff. We just laughed.

"About ten minutes later, the young man came in with the sheriff. I don't know what law we broke, but I guess the sheriff wanted to make sure there wasn't any big problem. As the sheriff came in, I recognized him, it was Hermilio Salinas, a big broad-shouldered guy we met many years before, and he like us, and we liked him. His name was Salinas, but he was no kin. He yelled out as he saw us, 'Juan, Tony how the hell are you? Man it's good to see you.' He walked up and gave each of us a big bear hug *abrazo*.

"At this, the young man's jaw popped down to his belt, and he was so disgusted and disappointed, he just walked out of the cantina cussing out the Salinases. I didn't feel bad 'cause I knew we didn't break no law."

In my travels driving Tío Juan around, we would come to this part of Momma's ranch and approach a huge mesquite tree about

The "Treaty Mesquite." Site of the Uvalde match

10 feet in circumference, and about 20 feet tall, and it would spark the following story. Later we called the tree Tío Juan's Mesquite Tree. Tío Juan told me that in 1933 he was working on horseback in deep northeast Webb County, before there were many fences. He said he and his men were camped under and around the tree. He was running about five hundred head of cattle on 12,000 acres. There were no cross fences. It turned out that the entire pasture was tick infested, and when ticks were detected, the state tick inspector insisted that he remove all the cattle and put them in quarantine. He had caught most of them, but still lacked about twenty cows.

He had a crew of nine cowboys with him. He said that day they got up before daybreak, cooked a quick breakfast, and got off on horseback just as the sun started to peek over the horizon.

South Texas cowboys learn quickly that you always get up before daybreak and start working. In Spanish, this is working *con la fresca de la mañana* (with the cool of the morning). You work hard before dawn, and take advantage of the cool, then try to break about noontime, then don't start until mid-afternoon to put in another 5 or 6 hours. Ideally, you do not have to work through the hottest part of the day, but you don't always get to take that luxury. Sometimes you have to work *de sol sale a sol se mete* (from sunup to sundown).

On that particular day, they rode for several hours, cutting for sign—zigzagging through acre after acre of brush country looking for cattle tracks on the dry dirt. They did not pick up sign until late afternoon. Later they were successful in catching all twenty head, and penning them at Las Abras Ranch, which Juan was leasing. Tío said they had a particularly hard time, the animals being wilder than usual, and much harder to catch. He said the activity drove them to about 10 miles east of Encinal, and they did not quit until about a half hour after sunset. Then they had the long ride back to camp, to the big mesquite. Ten men on horseback, in the dark, exhausted, sweated out, hungry, and fighting mosquitoes as big as swallows.

Juan said they made it back to camp after ten o'clock at night. There were three men waiting at the camp, sitting around the small campfire. The men were Bob Hall, the sheriff of Carrizo Springs; Sal Armstrong; and Sal's son, George Armstrong, friends of Juan's, and they had come to arrange a match roping between Juan and Toots Mansfield in Uvalde two weeks hence. They chatted and worked out the details of the match roping. Each man would rope six calves, and the one with the best time, the least amount of time, would win the roping, and the money.

After they made the deal, the men prepared to leave and drive back to Uvalde. As they got into their car, one of the men looked over at Juan in amazement and asked, "Juan, do you always work this late?" Juan started laughing, and the men joined him. He did not work that late every day, this day had been an exception, but the rodeo promoter obviously thought he had met the hardest-working man in rodeo. He did not work that late every day, but he was an extremely hardworking man. Nobody ever accused Juan Salinas of being lazy.

At the match roping in Uvalde, Juan met his opponent, a tall rawboned muscular young man named Toots Mansfield. Juan had heard that he was a good up-and-comer. However, Juan Salinas was still the hardest man to beat in South Texas. Prior to the start of the match, Juan was approached by a spokesperson of a group from Uvalde and was asked if he would bet on himself. Never being one to shy away from a bet and as a matter of fact a gambler most of his life, Juan agreed that he would bet $5,000 on himself. Tío Juan won the match. After the first match Ernest Lane, from Odem, Texas, just north of Corpus Christi, who trained horses for the King Ranch, a good friend who frequently bet on Juan, approached Juan. Ernest was a cotton farmer, rancher, and horse trainer. Ernest loved horses and was usually at any event that had horses, whether it be racing or roping. Ernest explained that the Uvalde group wanted revenge because Juan had won, and wanted a chance to win their money back. Juan was reluctant to put up the $10,000 bet. He confided to me that he wanted to take his money and run with it. However, he said he had to be a man about it, and bet on himself again. Ernest took $5,000 of the bet and Juan took the other $5,000. Again, Juan won the match, and another $5,000. By this time, the Uvaldeans were angry and insisted on another $10,000 bet. They pooled their money, and Ernest took another $5,000 and Juan another $5,000 of the bet. Juan won the third match. By that time the sun had set, there were no lights on the arena, and Juan was thankful that he did not have to prove his bravado one more time. He cooled off his horse, loaded him into the trailer and headed home for Encinal, having hit the richest afternoon he would ever experience in rodeo. Not only was Juan good with the loop, he also trained long hours for endurance. Imagine $15,000 in the middle of the depression—a fortune. Juan never beat Toots Mansfield again.

In 1936, Tío Juan was matched against Zack Sellers at the George Washington Birthday Celebration in Laredo, Texas. They each roped twenty calves. Tío said this type of roping favored him because while he might not be the quickest or fastest roper, he was among the most accurate. He rarely missed, even if it took him a little longer than others, and that did not happen too often. He won the bet money, and in addition won $1,000 put up by the rop-

Juan up on La India in a twenty-calf match against Zack Sellars,
1936. Laredo, Texas, Washington's Birthday Celebration

ing promoter. By pure coincidence in 2002, I was discussing this roping with C. O. "Chick" Rives, my ex-wife's uncle, who was born and raised in Laredo, and he responded, much to my surprise, that he remembered the roping very well. Tío Chick said that Juan had huge celebrity status by then. After the roping, Chick, then eleven years old, and other youngsters begged to walk and cool off Juan's horse. For no special reason Chick won the job. After walking the horse for about 30 minutes, Chick got the "princely sum of twenty-five cents." Forty years later, Tío Juan, Chick Rives, and their wives were at my wedding, and in 2004, I served as pallbearer at Tío Chick's funeral in Kerrville, Texas. Mid-morning on Saturday, my three sons and Tío Chick's sons C. O. and Andy, together with other nephews, dug out the grave with pick and shovel. The next day, we buried him at the cemetery in Sisterdale, Texas. Most of those in attendance participated in covering the casket with shovelfuls of dirt.

Several years later, after Tío Juan had teamed up with Toots Mansfield, Tío would experience another vengeance afternoon. Tío went to the Kincaid Hotel in Uvalde, Texas, where he said he did a lot of match roping business; many of his deals were struck at the Hotel. The deal was a roping in Carrizo Springs; Toots Mansfield was to be matched against Ted Powers from San Angelo. The roping and the bets were set, and Toots would be using Juan's horse. Tío said that one of the promoters was a man named Hal Ramsey, who was backing Ted Powers, and always bet against Tío and Toots.

The day of the contest came, and it was hot. Toots and Honey Boy did their thing, and won easily. After they lost, the Powers backers wanted a chance to get their money back, and insisted that Juan match rope against Zack Sellers, whom he had beaten in the Laredo roping in 1936. Juan and his friend Ernest Lane agreed to the match and bet money. It turned out that Zack Sellers was not in town, so Juan roped against Zack Sellers's father, Earl, and Juan beat him. A year or so later, there would be another roping in Uvalde between Juan and Zack Sellers and again Juan would be the winner.

A few other cowboys from the area made it on the circuit. Besides Tío Juan, Lem Reeves and Tom East; I know there was Ira Wood from Cotulla, and Dick Shelton from Tilden, a little town they call Dogtown, just east of Cotulla. I am sure there were many other ropers, dozens, perhaps hundreds, probably better than Juan, Lem, Tom, Ira, and Dick who just never got the breaks, did not have the money, the horse, and never got the chance to try the circuit.

The Brush Country produced another rodeo star, and that was Phil Lyne, predominantly a calf roper, but a master of all trades, from the Cotulla area. In 1973, Phil Lyne made it a point to try to beat Larry Mahan, who had been PRCA World All Around Champion Cowboy for several consecutive years. They competed all year, and in the end, Phil Lyne beat him; it was a tough, uphill battle but Phil did it. You can't get any higher in the rodeo ranks than World All Around Champion Cowboy. They competed in several events, including calf roping, bull riding, bronc riding, and other events, throughout the year. Sanctioned rodeos keep records and standings, and the winners are determined by the final competition, at the finals rodeo. There is a movie about this competition between Phil and Larry, titled *The Great American Cowboy*; it describes the yearlong fight for the top spot.

Tío told me that when his circuit companion Tom East died many years later, in the 1980s, they traveled to the East Ranch near Hebbronville, and that Phil Lyne and his wife took care of Tío and Tía, and helped them get around the place as the funeral took place. Tío said they had the funeral right there at the home, and buried Tom on a little bread-loaf hill just a short way from the house, and they had Tom's favorite horse, empty saddle up and ready, in the procession, and that the pallbearers were six of Tom's Tejano cowboys. It was very sad he said; there wasn't a dry eye in the place.

6

Juan Goes on the National Circuit

Having roped in every major rodeo in Texas for several years, not to mention all the small rodeos and match ropings, Juan was encouraged by those in the know, and those around him, to take the big step and go on the national circuit. The year was 1936. He was reluctant. Keep in mind that he was a high school dropout. He was no dummy for sure, but he was not an educated man. He spoke English but his vocabulary was limited, and he spoke with a marked Spanish accent. He asked friends and family for advice. His sister, Mucia, my mother, told me that he came to her. I guess he thought he should consult with the schoolteacher in the family. They talked for several hours; Momma encouraged him to go and try it, to venture out into the unknown, as there was very little he could lose. Juan always had plenty of pocket money, so in the worst of circumstances he would use his money to get home. In a 1983 interview, he stated that one of the main factors in making his decision was the miserable economy. As an example, he told of paying his cowboys $1 per day, for working from sunup to sundown. He said that there was simply no money, and no foreseeable way to make money.

His skills were honed to a sharp edge, and with the best horses he could find, a new car, and two friends, he was ready. With positive encouragement, Juan made plans to take off for his first national tour. He got a couple of rodeo friends to go with him—Tom East from Hebbronville, Texas, and Lem Reeves from Encinal. If ever there was a trio of tough cowboys from Texas, these were the men. Each was raised in the Brush Country around cattle, around tough men, around and on horses. Their work made them tough.

For the next ten years, Juan would rope with and beat the best. This also meant losing to the best, but he would win his share. The young man from the deep South Texas Brush Country would leave his mark on American rodeo forever.

Juan bought a new Chevrolet automobile, hooked up a two-horse trailer, and they were off. The first year Juan started in Dallas, then on to Shiner, Halletsville; Houston; then Beaumont; then rodeos in the southeastern states; then back to the Midwest; Nebraska; the Dakotas; Montana; Frontier Days in Cheyenne, Wyoming, the Daddy of all Rodeos; the Pendleton Round-Up; the Calgary Stampede; Denver and others in Colorado; New Mexico, Arizona; Nevada; then California; then hurried home to Encinal to check on the ranch operations and make plans and preparations to attend the Championship Rodeo at Madison Square Garden in New York City. Juan made the Championship Rodeo at Madison Square Garden ten consecutive years, from 1936 to 1946. This is incredible in and of itself, but for a small-town country boy, I never cease to be amazed. When you stop to think of it though, most cowboys come from tiny little towns, and started riding horses when still in diapers. Their talent elevated them to the big cities. Tío said he managed to get home to Encinal to check on things once or twice a year.

Tío explained that in 1936 he first went to Dallas and did not win a penny. Then he traveled to Shiner where there was a four-day rodeo, and he won everything. He said they gave a beautiful engraved saddle to the roper with the best time on eight calves, four in tie-down roping, and four in breakaway roping. He won the saddle; he explained that a good saddle was a cherished prize in those days. After the Shiner Rodeo, he went to Halletsville, where he won some, then on to points beyond.

After touring the nation throughout the year, the last two rodeos he attended were held in the east: the World Championship Rodeo in New York's Madison Square Garden in late October, and the Championship Rodeo in Boston Garden. Tío Juan had instructions on where to go when he arrived in New York City. He was to get to Manhattan, then drive straight into the downtown area, find Madison Square Garden, then find the entrance to the basement. He had a map someone had given him, scrawled on a piece of paper. It makes me cry thinking of my Mexican boy Tío Juan driving in the middle of Manhattan in his Chevrolet, pulling his two-horse trailer, trying to find a parking place. If you have ever been in Manhattan and have seen the skyscrapers and the multitudes of people, you know what I mean.

He found the entrance, and was amazed to find the entire basement of the Garden transformed into an underground stable. All the rodeo animals, the bulls, the broncs, the calves and steers, were kept in the basement, and the contestants' horses were kept there also. They unloaded their horses, feed, saddles, and equipment, and were ready for the rodeo. They found a hotel nearby and enjoyed the several-day stay. Tío said that the first year he went to New York, he paid $100 a week for his hotel; the last year, ten years later, the same accommodations cost $300 per week.

Tío talked about taking advantage of the stay in New York City, and attending as many sports events and games as he could. Not only was he an athlete in his own sport, but he also loved other sports: baseball, basketball, and football in particular.

One evening in the early 1990s, we watched *Monday Night Football* on TV. The game was at Soldier Field in Chicago. When the sportscaster mentioned they were in Chicago, Tío surprised me when he said, "I roped there many times. They prepared a roping arena on the football field, and we had a huge rodeo. That was the longest rope in the whole U.S. They let the calf go for a long time before we could start the chase. If you start too early, they penalize you five seconds. Some places they penalize more. There were no set rules yet. I guess they wanted more people to see the action, so they made us chase longer. Of course, everybody had longer times." He said the same about the Coliseum in Los Angeles. He told a story about a huge rodeo in San Francisco: One of the cowboys, a friend of his, was in love with a famous and very rich fan dancer, Sally Rand. She was a movie star, a celebrity, she loved her cowboy, and all the cowboys got an invitation to their wedding. Tío said all the cowboys and cowgirls went to the huge wedding and reception in Oakland, across the bay. Tío did not remember the name of the cowboy.

Tío mentioned that all the big rodeos had the top country-western musicians and entertainers in the country. He told me many times what a good friend Gene Autry became. He said Gene sang at many rodeos and the same for Roy Rogers. I have photos of Autry and Rogers at the early day rodeos. I also have an auto-graphed photo of Tío Juan and Tía Bertha with Roy Rogers.

One day I flew with Tío Juan to Houston to see an eye doctor. As we drove in a cab right in the middle of downtown Houston, he said, "The Arena was right about here, and I roped here many, many times. Them was the days before the Astrodome." After these comments, I was in awe that the sport and his ability had taken him right to the heart of athletics in America. He would often say that being a baseball, basketball, or football player could not compare to being a rodeo performer. "All they have to do is show up, hell, I gots to travel thousands of miles driving my car, pulling my horses, I have to bring my own equipment, and feed for my horses, and it was not an easy thing."

When Tío, Lem, and Tom walked the streets of New York City, young men who were not used to seeing cowboys heckled them. "Hey, hillbilly, hey Zeke, hey plowboy, hey big fancy cow-boy," were some of the jeers. They took it as they walked along. Tío Juan said that to be honest, they were somewhat scared. They were in one of the biggest cities in the world, all the way from the South Texas Brush Country, and they didn't know what to say, or what to do. Finally, Lem could not stand it. One young boy got in Lem's face and teased him, "Hey big, strong, tough cowboy, just like in the movies." It was all Lem could take; he grabbed the young boy, threw him to the ground, and beat him up good. They had to pull Lem off the boy to keep him from getting into trouble. Tío said that whenever cowboys were in any town and the locals wanted trouble they would find it, and regret it for sure. The city boys made a mistake of thinking that these boot-tough cowboys were the movie guys they saw at the Saturday matinee. These men threw two- and three-hundred-pound calves, roped, tugged, and knocked down bulls, had horses fall on them, and did it in the hot South Texas sun, day in and day out. When you stop and think, there probably were not many other men whose occupations made them tougher. In retrospect, I suppose the city fellows thought these cowboys were regular people walking around in Halloween costumes. They made a mistake.

At the Garden Finals after World War II, during a lull in the action, one young bull rider asked Lem Reeves why he had not fought in the war. Lem took this as an insult. He felt the bull rider was insinuating that he was chicken and had evaded the draft. Lem took out after the young boy, whipped him, and then walked back to where he was sitting saying, "that's why I didn't go to the war, 'cause I would've whipped all the enemy, including Hitler, and the war would've been over. And I would of done it quickly, just like I took care of you." All the cowboys roared.

In putting the final touches on this book, I wrote Lem's family in Freer, Texas, asking for photos. I got a response from his daughter Jesse Neese, who sent various items. One was an article from the *Alice Echo-News Journal*, dated April 1, 1992, a feature story on Lem's niece Linda Sue Henley, who had a cowboy art studio in Helotes, Texas. She tells the following story on her uncle Lem Reeves. "She describes Lem as the epitome of a real cowboy and credits him for the name of her studio. One of her favorite tales goes back to the 1940s, when Lem was in the Championship Rodeo at New York's Madison Square Garden. He and another cowboy had a disagreement that ended with blows at Dempsey's Bar. With one good right, Lem took this taller and bigger fellow out. As his peers and friends gathered around to ask how he managed it, Lem casually raised his arm, clenched his fist and coolly stated, 'With a Little Bit of Texas.' And the name of the studio? Little Touch of Texas Art Studio, of course."

I did not meet Lem until the late 1950s at a hunting camp on Momma's ranch. He was up in years, but you could tell he was still a tough guy. I heard later that several years after that he had fallen about 50 feet, off an oil field drilling rig; he survived and lived a long life thereafter. Tough guy, indeed.

Tío told me about fighting tough cowboys. "They was always one or two cowboys that loved to fight. I remember especially the McCrory brothers from Deadwood, South Dakota. They was always fighting. Most of the fights was always in the bars, saloons, cantinas. *Pleitos de cantina*, barroom fights. In Nueva Yorka, one cowboy killed this fellow in a barroom fight. The peoples running the rodeo and the Madison Square Garden peoples, they tried to help the cowboy, and he got off, on self-defense, they didn't bring any charges against him. They just told him, 'next year when you come, use another name.' Then there was another huge fight in Boston one year. Another cowboy, he killed another fellow. These guys loved to fight, and they didn't use no knives or guns, they just fought with their fists. They loved to fight, and Lem he was one of them guys loved to fight, but he never kill nobody. Thank God, or maybe he never come back to Texas, we have to leave him up there." Tío laughed aloud.

On a drive through the ranch, Tío explained about New York. He always called it Nueva Yorka. "The finals rodeo was always in Nueva Yorka. Then years later, they changed it to Oklahoma City then to Las Vegas. I went to Vegas a couple of times as a spectator. It was about the same—big city lots of peoples, except in Vegas they got lots of whores, lots more than Nueva Yorka, and of course the gambling casinos." They still hold the finals in Las Vegas.

One of the best things that could have happened to Tío Juan happened in Beaumont, Texas, in 1936. He met and fell in love with a beautiful young woman. Her name was Bertha Hargraves, and she was a beauty. Tía Bertha told us many years later that she had told her dad she had met the man she wanted to marry, and would he please take her around to the rodeos around Beaumont. He did take her around, and she and Juan got to know each other, and they were married in 1936. Being on the road, it was kind of a quick marriage. They got married, and that year he went on following the rodeo action for the next several months, and she stayed home in Beaumont. Traveling with the rodeo was not in the plans

Mrs. Juan L. Salinas (née Bertha Hargraves).
Married Juan Salinas in 1936

for Bertha for that year. Juan finished several rodeos, then came home to Encinal, then sent for Bertha. Tía Bertha said he sent her money to come on the train, and that the train took her to San Antonio first, then south to Encinal. She told me that the first family member she met was my daddy, Abe Palacios Sr., at the Encinal depot. Juan had to work that day, and asked Dad to go meet her and bring her to the home ranch. Juan met his young bride that evening for supper. You think Juan would have made plans to meet his one and only, but work came first for the cowboy. For the next several years, Juan and Bertha lived at the Salinas Ranch with Mamá Minnie. Tía Bertha called her mother-in-law Miss Salinas, or Mamá Minnie.

Tío Juan and Tía Bertha never had children. Actually, she had a tubal pregnancy a couple of years after they married, and was never able to become pregnant again. It was sad that such powerful people and personalities would never have offspring, but on the positive side, this allowed her to accompany Juan on his decade-long trek.

Tío talked about the many rodeos held in small isolated towns. He said that many of the cowboys and their families set up camp near the arena, with tents and campfires. They slept there, cooked, and ate at the campsites. In many of the arenas, there were no bleachers, and cars parked around the arena at right angles. In the bigger towns or cities the cowboys stayed in hotels or motels, or as they were known then, tourist courts.

Tío said that after a year or two they stayed at the same hotels or same apartments, and the clerks and managers got to know them well. Tía Bertha prepared a wooden box with kitchen utensils, pots, and pans and left them in storage at a small apartment in Manhattan, near Madison Square Garden. As the time neared for the trip north, they would call the landlord, and let him know they were on the way. When they arrived, they got their wooden box.

After the first couple of years, Tío Juan decided to start the circuit in California every year, to avoid the foggy highways of the Gulf Coast in the wintertime, thus he would progress from west to east, since in those years the championship rodeos were always at Madison Square Garden in Manhattan.

In 1995, I took over Tío's ranch, his house, and his P.O. Box 45 in Encinal. I still get an invitation from the rodeo at Sidney, Iowa. The leaflet is now addressed to Ivan Salinas. Through the years, the "Juan" has deteriorated to "Ivan". I also get brochures from Cheyenne Frontier Days and from Nebraska's Big Rodeo in Burwell, Nebraska.

Ernest Lane liked Juan and sought him out at every rodeo. They got together for meals and drinking before and after all the rodeos. Ernest always bet on Juan, and won a lot of money betting on him. One day in the mid-1930s Ernest called Juan at his home in Encinal to tell him that Ernest's wife and a blacksmith had won a quarter horse gelding in a raffle in Robstown, Texas. Ernest said that he could buy the blacksmith out if Juan wanted to try the horse. Juan was in need of another good horse so he told Ernest to go ahead and get the horse. That weekend Ernest showed up at the Salinas Ranch near Encinal with the horse, and Juan liked what he saw. He walked the horse around, saddled him, tried him out for a few minutes, and then told Ernest he wanted him. Tío asked Ernest how much he wanted for him, and Ernest told him there was no charge. It was a gift from Ernest. When Tía Bertha saw the young horse, she loved him too, and came up and started petting him and cooing at him and calling him Honey Boy. The name stuck, it was Honey Boy.

Honey Boy turned out to be one of the best calf roping horses in rodeo history. You talk to rodeo people today and bring up the subject of good horses, and you will inevitably hear the name Honey Boy. Read about rodeo horses, and you are bound to read about Honey Boy. Every couple of years or so the horse and rodeo magazines run an article on Honey Boy. Juan took Honey Boy with him everywhere he went for the remainder of his career. Honey Boy died at the Salinas Ranch in Encinal, in 1955.

Tío Juan had several fine rodeo horses. Stormy was another famous Salinas horse that Juan raised from a colt at the ranch; he named it Hitler. During the war, rodeo promoters thought the name Hitler inappropriate, and insisted he use another "stage" name. He was renamed Stormy because he had been born on a stormy night. Another, and one of the best—probably just as good as Honey Boy—was the mare La India, who rated way up there with Honey Boy as an excellent roping horse. She too was born and raised on the Salinas Ranch. She was named for one of Tío Tony's

Juan Salinas coming off Honey Boy, Sidney, Iowa, 1938

girlfriends who was nicknamed La India. After her roping days, La India became a brood mare. Juan said he sold many of La India's foals at a handsome price. His friends quickly added that he probably sold about one hundred of La India's offspring—biologically impossible, of course. Another excellent roping mare raised on the ranch was La Irene, also named after one of Tío Tony's girlfriends.

Tío said, "I gotta tell you this story about La India. We was at the Boston Garden, we was getting warmed up, Clyde Burk he rode up on his horse, and I was riding La India. He said 'Juan, I bet you one hundred dollars you can't rope off your horse without reins.' I said I'd take the bet. So, when I got the first calf, I took the bridle and reins off La India, and backed her up into the box with my feet, pushing on the stirrups. Then when I was ready I called for my calf, took off, and when I roped the calf, I sat back in my saddle and yelled out as loud as I could, 'Whoaaa,' and pulled on her mane, and she stopped like she would with reins, and I got off and tied up. I didn't win the roping, but I made money, and I beat Clyde, and he had to pay me one hundred dollars."

Tom East was kin to the Klebergs from the King Ranch in Kingsville, and had an aunt who lived in one of the finer hotels in New York City. On the way up to New York, Tom was sometimes short of cash. Tío Juan explained that like so many ranching families, including the Salinases, the Easts were land poor. Tom

Juan Salinas and Honey Boy

loved to calf rope, and accompanied Tío to many rodeos. Even Juan attributed his launch into national roping to the poor cash situation at the ranch. There was plenty of land, plenty of food and cattle, but very little cash. It was not an affluent society. Because of this, sometimes Juan paid all expenses, and even Tom's entry fees and room and board. After the group settled at the Garden, Tom would excuse himself and go off to see his aunt. After a day or so Tom returned, and he would announce to all that his sweet aunt had given him plenty of pocket change, and Tom even bragged about it and told everybody that they were in the chips. There was plenty of party money for the remainder of the stay.

Tío elaborated on the lack of cash and affluence. "Nobody had any money, there was no cash, and there were no credit cards. Banks only loaned money to the wealthy, usually to purchase land or other large assets. I can take you right now to two ranchitos where people lost either the land or the minerals. One old man

La India

lost his small ranch because he couldn't pay his groceries; he told
the grocer he would pay later but the grocer made him deed over
the ranch. When he tried to pay the grocery bill, the grocer didn't
want the cash; he kept the ranchito. The other was a fellow lost his
minerals to a lumber company, the same thing happen; he needed
lumber, had no cash, could not pay; the lumberyard guy insisted
on something, and got the minerals. That wasn't as bad as losing
the ranch, because those minerals have never produced, but the
guy still lost something. Times were hard."

Tom East went on tour with Juan for several years. They had
been friends from area ropings and matches in Texas. As the years
passed, their friendship strengthened; they became very good

Ready for action, Sidney, Iowa. Left to right: Toots
Mansfield, Clyde Burk, Juan Salinas

friends. Years later, anytime that Juan needed a new horse or stud
horse, he took Tom up on this standing offer to send over horseflesh. Over the years, Tom sent Tío Juan over half a dozen horses.
Juan offered to pay, but Tom would take no payment. The last
horse Tom sent was in the late 1970s. The stud was El Moto out of
Ranchero Lady 32, by Ranchero. El Moto gave Juan many ponies
and fillies over the years. Today we still have two horses from El
Moto, a fifteen-year-old named Calcetines (Socks), and a young
pony born the day Tía Bertha died, in 1991, which we appropriately
named Bert.

I asked Tío once what he liked most about his life as a rancher.
He responded, "The thing I like the best about my life on the ranch
was the horses. Horses are so beautiful. I loved horses. I loved to
ride them, to raise them, and I even entered many races with my
own horses. When Laredo started having races at LIFE (Laredo
International Fair and Exposition Downs), I was a field judge.
Many years ago, my friend Ernest Lane from Odem was training
quarter horses for the King Ranch. Ernest had this one great little
mare named Miss Princess that was burning the tracks in Mexico

(above) Sheu Fly and Miss Princess, Del Rio, 1947.
Ernest Lane, left; Bob Kleberg, far right

and South Texas. Only trouble was another mare from Louisiana named Sheu Fly was winning all the races in Texas, and held all the time records. Sooner or later, the two mares were gonna race. It was 1947, and I got a call from Ernest. He told me that the day had come that Miss Princess was going to race Sheu Fly at Del Rio, Texas. I got all excited because I wanted to see the race. I had heard about both mares, and they was both very fast. Both mares had good reputations for being very fast. Bertha and I, we went to the race, and the day before the race, the promoters put up a purse of $30,000, then Ernest and the owners and others placed their side bets; they gave me the side bet bag to take to the hotel to hold for the next day. I brought a bag full of about $50,000 cash to the motel room, and wondered if I was gonna get conked on the head and held up that night. Nothing happened that night. The race was held the next day. It was a beautiful race. Miss Princess won, and went on to win World Champion. It was a beautiful race—I never will forget it."

I have been around horses most of my life. Not deeply involved, but there's always been a horse either at home or at the ranch. Dad always had a horse at home from the time I was about ten until I went to college. I have read volumes on horses, horse raising, horse training, and anything "horse". I am amazed at how generous horsemen are with their horses. Ernest Lane mentions in *The King Ranch Quarter Horses*, by Robert Moorman Denhardt, that Bob Kleberg, one of the principals at the King Ranch, *gave* him the horse Top Deck. Later Ernest sold Top Deck for $25,000. Ernest *gave* Honey Boy to Tío Juan. Then for years, Tom *gave* Tío horses, as he needed. Tío *gave* Toots Mansfield his horse, Muffin. I have heard of many occasions when horsemen gave horses to others.

7

Circuit Experiences

After two years of working the national rodeos, Juan still kept roping the local and area rodeos, and met up again with Toots Mansfield, whom he had beaten that one afternoon in Uvalde a couple of
years earlier. Juan ran into him at all the South Texas ropings, and
admired the young man. Juan could tell that he was a cut above the
rest of the ropers, and that he was taller and stronger than most,
and particularly good at flanking big calves.

One afternoon after a roping in Cotulla, Texas, Toots approached Juan about sponsoring him in professional rodeo. Juan
had never sponsored anyone, and he himself had no sponsor, but
he knew the deal. The sponsor would pay all expenses, and provide
horse and equipment if necessary and would split the winnings
fifty-fifty. Juan decided to take a risk.

Momma told me that Toots moved to the Salinas Ranch for a
couple of months. There the men practiced at the arena a couple of
hundred yards from the house. The practice was intense, and took
place every day. Momma was teaching in the one room school just
next to the arena at the time. She said she remembered the practice
sessions vividly. All she and the students had to do was look out
the window to see the ropers 50 yards away.

As I prepared to finish this book I contacted Lem Reeves's
daughter Jesse Neese in Freer, and she told me of her Mother's re-
cent death. She mentioned going through her things and that she
had found a baby girl's dress, still kept in a gift box, with a gift card
inside, signed with best wishes by my mother Mucia. I can imagine

Tony Salinas in action, late 1930s

that while the ropers and their families were at the Salinas Ranch preparing to go on the circuit, they got to know each other well.

After many weeks of intense practice at the Salinas arena, it was time to go; they packed up and headed north on the circuit. They returned to South Texas every three or four months. Packing meant taking whatever they thought they would need: clothing, bedding, food, and water. They also had the horses, La India the first several years, then Honey Boy, and all the saddles and other equipment, gear, and feed.

Juan told me that Toots stood out as a darned good roper, particularly in flanking large calves, but he had no idea that Toots was as good as he was. When it was all over and done about ten years later, Toots had won seven World Championship Calf Roping titles. Juan made a lot of money with Toots. Toots was very grateful for the opportunity. When Juan took him on, there was no way he could get into the game, as he had no money, no top quality horse, and no equipment. Sad to say a young man has to part with a percentage of his winnings, but it is still part of the game today, as it is in other sports. Around others and me, Tío called Toots "Patas Largas" (Long Legs).

Toots Mansfield was inducted into the Texas Sports Hall of Fame in 1995. In an article in the *Fort Worth Star-Telegram*, the newspaper gave the following statistics: Toots won his first World

Championship in 1939. From 1939 to 1951, Toots was either the world champion or runner up. He won seven World Championships at Madison Square Garden, he won the Pendleton Round-Up three times, Frontier Days in Cheyenne three times, and the Southwestern at Fort Worth four times. To give you an idea, he won $21,300 in 1948. In 1947, he won a winner-take-all steer-roping purse of $14,500.

Toots was vice president of the Turtle Association, then president when the name changed to the Rodeo Cowboys Association in 1945. He was president every year until 1951. He came out of retirement in 1955 because the cattle business had gotten so bad. At age forty-one, he still placed third in the rankings.

I purchased a book the other day titled *Fifty Years of Nebraska's Big Rodeo*. It is a historical compilation of the Big Rodeo in Burwell, Nebraska, one of the biggest rodeos in the nation. The statistics show that in the late 1930s and early 1940s, Tío Juan, Tío Tony, and Toots Mansfield took turns in the first, second, and third places in the calf roping.

In addition to sponsoring Toots, Juan roped, and occasionally won big. He said he won his share of ropings and beat the field; he just did not win as often as the champions did. In an interview I taped in 1983, he said that at one time he probably ranked third in the world. He said his winnings averaged about $30,000 per year for the ten years he was on the circuit. In addition, he rented out Honey Boy and took half of the winnings if the winner used Honey Boy. He told me he rented Honey Boy to a roper from out west once, and the cowboy won the roping, but did not pay Juan. He told Tío he would send him a check when he got home to Oklahoma. Tío said he never expected payment, but after he got home to Encinal, in a couple of days a check for half the winnings came in the mail. "Overall, I averaged about $30,000 per year including bets, fees, and splits, during the ten years I was on the circuit, from 1936 to 1946. Aside from Toots, I also had a couple other cowboys that worked for me short term, Jake McClure, Jack Skipworth, Royce Sewalt, Jack Shaw, and Bus Seaberry." Not bad, considering it was just after the Great Depression, then into World War II.

Tío was also a gambler; in addition to the established sources of income, Juan loved to bet, and he bet on Honey Boy, Toots, or any other sure thing he could find. He always took conservative bets, those he could win. He lost sometimes, but not often. He mentioned that one week it had rained heavily and they could not rope. The men decided to run foot races. Tío Tony entered the contest, and Juan bet heavily knowing that Tony was a superior athlete and never lost a foot race. Tony ran the 100-yard dash in ten flat, and sometimes broke ten.

Tony was ten years younger than Juan and was just barely out of high school when he began competing on the circuit. He had played sports in high school, and on many occasions roped wearing a baseball cap and tennis shoes. In the local or area rodeos this was acceptable, but in the RCA or PRCA sanctioned rodeos, if you wanted to compete with the cowboys, you absolutely had to dress like the cowboys. Rodeo officials reminded Tony that he must wear a cowboy hat and boots, or he could not compete. The image was important for the promotion of the rodeo and marketing of the event. Today, a rodeo star wearing a baseball cap and boots might attract more people than one wearing the cookie cutter hat and boots, but then who knows where it would end— no shirts, long hair, dreadlocks, corn rows? It is a good rule and should continue.

The promoter of the New York Championship Rodeo insisted that the men wear cowboy clothes, and at least for certain functions and events that the men wear a tie with their regular clothes. Tío told me that the promoter insisted they wear ties to show the public that they were professional athletes and could behave and appear like gentlemen, and not just a bunch of rowdy cowpunchers from the hinterland. To those in the know, the coat and tie did not change a thing.

I am very fortunate to have many of the New York Championship Rodeo photos. These are panoramic photos taken either at the basement of Madison Square Garden or at the steps of City Hall in New York City. In some of these, some of the men are wearing neckties.

I am also fortunate to have about thirty number badges that
Tío Juan and others wore. These are either round or square flan-
nel patches, each with a number, and some with the name of the
rodeo, and the year imprinted on the edge. Cowboys wore them
on their upper arm, or somehow fastened to their back; this was
their identifying number. I also have metal pin-on badges, some
of these are from Madison Square Garden; Buffalo Championship
Rodeo; Boston Garden; Nebraska's Big Rodeo, Burwell; Houston Fat Stock Show, Rodeo and Horse Show; and San Antonio,
Southwestern Exposition & Fat Stock Show and Rodeo. I also
have many photos of their trips around the United States, Juan and
Toots, Juan with the stars of the day, Bob Crosby, Jack Skipworth,
Clyde Burke, Homer Pettigrew, Jake McClure, and many others.

Tío Juan was especially proud of one New York City Hall panoramic with Mayor Fiorello La Guardia in the front row in the
middle. "I got to meet the mayor and shake his hand. He asked me
if I was *Italiano*, and I said no, I'm Mexicano, and he just said "Oh",
and laughed."

Tío told a story about driving toward Burwell, Nebraska, one
night with Toots. They were still about 60 miles away at sunset.
They drove through a small town and decided to get a motel room,
and get an early start in the morning. They found an empty lot next
to the motel, and tethered and hobbled the horses for the night.

They awoke the next morning, went to breakfast and prepared
for the trip into Burwell. When they went to get the horses, a
man wearing a coat, tie, and fedora was waiting for them by the
horses. When he saw them, he started cussing them out, because
according to the man, the horses were stinking up the lot, and the
man's funeral home was right next to the empty lot. The man kept
berating them, and complaining about the horse droppings and
the accompanying smell, explaining that his clients were going to
think his funeral home smelled. He kept after them, as they led
the horses onto the trailer, and loaded the equipment. Tío made
sure the women were in the car and the car ready to go. All this
time the funeral director kept yakking at them.

Finally, Juan asked Toots, "Are you ready to go?" Toots answered that he was. Juan started to get in behind the wheel, and the funeral director kept following him, still complaining and now screaming. Juan finally looked at him seriously, leaned back a little, and hit the funeral man right in the chops with a right cross. The hat went one way, the man went down the other way, Juan slid behind the wheel and the Chevrolet and trailer headed out of town. They kept waiting for the law to catch up to them and pull them over, but it never happened. After several miles, they burst out laughing.

I talked to Toots several years ago and asked him about racism in the rodeo ranks. He mentioned that like any organization there were always some racists, but generally, they left one another alone. He compared rodeo to a professional football or baseball team. Everyone is a professional athlete, respects one another, and with very few exceptions is very tolerant. He mentioned to me that he never saw any discriminatory action. Juan and Tony were the only Hispanic performers at most rodeos and everyone accepted them. In fact, the peer group of cowboys embraced them, and they returned the sentiment.

Tío Juan told me of one incident at a Texas match roping on a hot afternoon. Tío Juan was the main attraction. After a few calves were roped, Tío worked his horse into the box, and the announcer called out that Juan Salinas from Encinal, Texas, was preparing to come out of the box to rope a calf. A spectator who sat directly in front of Tía Bertha, who just happened to have a beer bottle in her hand, made a rank comment like, Aw hell, here comes that damn Mexican again. Tía Bertha broke the beer bottle on his head. An altercation ensued, but luckily, no action was taken against her. Word got around about the incident, and everybody knew you did not say anything negative about Tío Juan if you were sitting close to Tía Bertha.

As I said in my opening comments, Juan Salinas went where no Mexican had gone before and few have gone since. We will never know precisely why the Salinases had no problem with race and discrimination, but they never did. This was true not only in places

Juan and Bertha Salinas, Grand Canyon, 1939

where Mexicans and the racist issues were not present like New York City and Boston, but in Texas itself. In San Antonio, Corpus Christi, Houston, Dallas, Fort Worth, and other cities, it was the same. There might be race issues in each of these cities, but the Salinases never had any problems. Fort Worth has been criticized for ignoring its Mexican population and pretending it does not exist. This may be true, but Juan and Tony rodeoed there for many years, at the Southwestern Exposition and Fat Stock Show Rodeo. I have a photo of Tío Juan and Tía Bertha, at Forth Worth's Texas Hotel in 1940, where they attended a banquet for the Cowboys Turtle Association. Maybe most Mexicans could only get into the Texas Hotel through the back door, but Juan walked in through the front door, and dined in the main ballroom, as one of the stalwarts of the rodeo profession, and nobody said or did anything about it.

The irony of the situation is almost humorous. The Hispanic whose ancestors had brought horses, cattle, and all things cowboy and rodeo to America was at times the attraction that brought spectators to spend a buck or two and watch the Hispanic rope. As Juan said, "they never seen no Mexican boy throw a loop, so they come to watch me. They paid at the gate to come watch me."

After Juan and Toots became popular rodeo stars, they contracted to model for the Montgomery Ward catalog in the shirt and pant section. I vaguely remember Momma bringing the catalog home, and showing me the page where Tío Juan and Toots were modeling clothes. Juan was wearing his trademark white shirt and khaki pants. Product endorsements already existed back then, but nothing compared to the present day millions that sponsors pay athletes to tout their products.

In addition, there was one other perk that Tío received, and that was a brand new pair of Justin pointy boots any time he wanted. He always wore the cockroach stompers, the pointy toes, never tried the round toes, and always wore the riding heel, never the walking heel. He got new boots when he wanted, and he was thrilled to go by the post office and get his free pair of boots.

From this experience, Juan developed a lifelong habit of asking for payment when he was photographed. Every time someone

It is hereby understood and agreed that on this day,
November 6, 1936, the undersigned cowboys and cowgirls have formed an
association to be called The United Cowboys Turtle Association, and do hereby
agree to abide by the rules and regulations thereof, as stipulated in the
following clauses:

Rule No.1.   Any cowboy or cowgirl will be assessed and required to pay
$500.00 to the Association to reenter the Union if he or she performs or
competes in that particular rodeo where a strike is called. The reentry
of said strike-breakers must be voted upon by silent vote by all members of
the Turtle Association.

Rule No. 2. The $500.00 paid to the United Cowboys Turtle Association by
the strike-breakers or violators of the association will go to a trust fund,
to be used for lawyer fees, telephone calls, telegrams, or for a representative to be sent to any rodeo committee, which the Cowboys Association agrees
is offering insufficient and unfair purses. It is further understood and
agreed that a fine of $100.00 must be paid to the Association by any cowgirl
or cowboy for disgraceful conduct, which must be proven before the Board of
Directors.

It is to be the ruling of this organization that each member
shall be assessed a yearly fee of $5.00, which will go into the trust fund,
to be put into a bank that is agreeable to all members of the Association.
It is further understood that no one member of this organization may check
upon this fund. All checks must be signed by at least four members of the
Board of Directors or officials. No representative, speaker or member of
the Board of Directors is to be paid a salary for his services. This is to
be given free of charge to the organization.

It is also understood that a representative must be present at
that certain rodeo on which a strike is called, and be able to prove that any
member of this association has competed at that certain rodeo.

Rule No. 3. Strikes are not to be called by any one member of this
association, because he or she may be dissatisfied by the decision of the
judges, rules and regulations, or by finding fault with the committee or
prize list, but must be passed upon by all members of the association, and
if it is passed upon, a representative is to go to the committee with a
list signed by all of the members.   After a member has once signed his or
her name to this list, the association has the right to use his name on any
list that is to be sent to a rodeo committee where the purses are considered
unsatisfactory and unfair.   No one person has the right to send in a list
that is not approved by all the members of this organization, and should
anyone do this, he or she will be expelled from this association, and will
be assessed the $500.00 as stipulated in Rule No.1 to reenter the Union.

Rule No. 4. It is not the rule of this organization to interfere with
personal disagreements among members, nor with personal demands of a cowboy
for his rights. For instance: Should a show have a judge who is thought
unfair in his decisions, a cowboy has the right to demand a fair deal,
without the interference of the Association. The Union has a right to demand
capable and fair judges, and should there be judges who do not come up to
this standard, the Union reserves the right to send a representative to the
rodeo committee to ask for a change of judges.

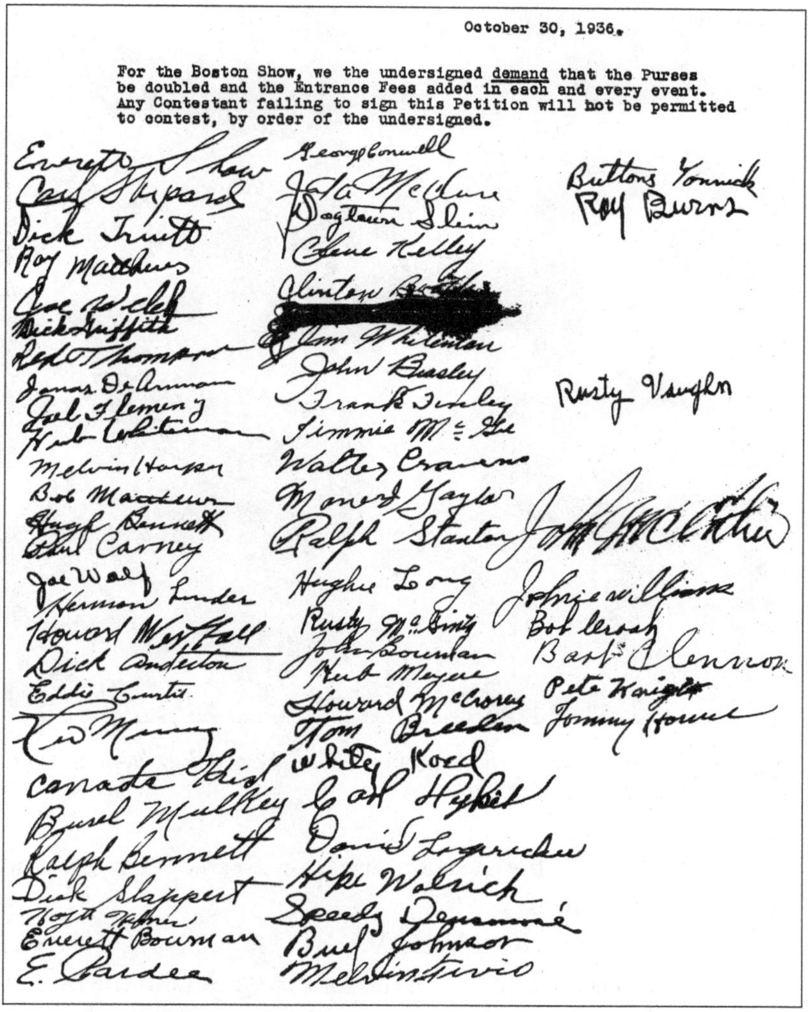

October 30, 1936.

For the Boston Show, we the undersigned <u>demand</u> that the Purses be doubled and the Entrance Fees added in each and every event. Any Contestant failing to sign this Petition will hot be permitted to contest, by order of the undersigned.

Above: Petition to the promoter of the Boston rodeo, October 30, 1936. Signed by many of Juan Salinas's friends and fellow rodeo performers. From the Estelle Gilbert Papers, Box 1, Folder 9, courtesy Dickinson Research Center, National Cowboy & Western Heritage Museum, Oklahoma City, Okla.

Left: Articles of Association By-Laws and Rules of the United Cowboys Turtle Association, the forerunner organization of the Professional Rodeo Cowboys' Association (PRCA). From Booklets and Pamphlets, Box 14, Folder 9. Courtesy Dickinson Research Center, National Cowboy & Western Heritage Museum, Oklahoma City, Okla.

Cowboy Turtles Association Banquet, Hotel Texas, Fort Worth, 1940

asked to take a snapshot, he shot forward with an open right hand
and said, *paga primero* (pay first).

A couple of years after World War II, Tío Juan and Tío Tony
took Luis Soto from Encinal on the tour to work with the horses,
keep them fed and watered, watch the equipment and other odd
jobs around the arena. Tío Tony and Luis liked their whiskey and
beer. One day at Madison Square Garden, Tío Juan showed up at
the area designated for them in the basement, and Luis and Tío
Tony had not done the necessary cleanup and chores. Tío looked
closely and noticed that they were both somewhat glassy-eyed. He
knew from experience that they had been hitting the joy juice. Tío
Juan got angry, searched around the car and equipment and found
two bottles of bourbon. He took the two bottles over to a concrete
drain and broke them against each other, much to the pain and

disgust of Luis and Tío Tony. Luis still lives in Encinal where he is a retired electrician. He tells stories about his trips around the country with the Salinas brothers. Luis distinguished himself as an infantry soldier in the European theater during World War II.

Luis told me an interesting story about a big Encinal cattleman. "This old man asked me to go with him to San Antonio, just so he wouldn't go alone. I thought it was a good idea, so I went with him. We went and he bought some bulls, and some hardware and stuff like that. At night, we went to a nice hotel, and he got two rooms, one for him and one for me.

"At about midnight, I heard a commotion next door in the cattleman's room. He had arranged that I had a door to his room in case he needed help. I heard more and more noise, so I opened the door to the room, and there was the cattleman paying the bellhop

Toots Mansfield, relaxing on the road

Front row, left to right: Irv Montgomery, Bertha Salinas,
Juan Salinas, James Kenney. Standing: Roy Rogers

for another bottle of whiskey. There were several empty bottles of beer and whiskey lying all over the floor, and the cattleman had taken off a money belt he was wearing, and there was money, hundred dollar bills scattered all over the room.

"The cattleman kept telling the bellhop to take as much of it as he wanted. He was in no pain. I told the bellhop to leave. I gathered all the money, and put it back in the money belt. By the time I finished gathering all the money, the cattleman was asleep. I put the money belt in his suitcase and went back to my room. In the morning, I got up and went downstairs for breakfast. The cattleman was all dressed up and reading the newspaper in the lobby. We went to breakfast. Nothing was ever said about the money and the bottles".

After a couple of trips east, Juan knew the territory like his own South Texas country. He told me that when they got close to New York City every year, they made plans to go to Plymouth, Mas-

Madison Square Garden, 1939. Juan Salinas,
lower left corner (in black shirt and tie)

sachusetts, and find a certain hardware store. At the store, they
bought several cans of manila rope, the rope they used for their
roping. Today ropers use some sort of poly plastic, or fiberglass
ropes. Back then, all the ropers used the yellow natural fiber or
sisal type ropes. Somehow, Juan found out that he could buy the
rope in wholesale quantities, and he stocked up every year on the
way to the Boston Garden. The rope came in 5-gallon tin cans, and

he bought four or five every year. "Manila rope from Plymouth, Massachusetts."

In 1939, after the Championship Rodeo in New York City, a promoter organized a group of cowboys to go to England and put on a number of rodeos. They went by boat, with livestock and all. The promoter asked Tío to go two or three times, but Tío declined. "I wanted to go across the ocean, but I never did go. I wanted to get on back to Encinal to check on my cows, horses, and my peoples. Later I hear that things did not go too well. They made a number of rodeos but there wasn't too much money. I could have said I had been overseas to Europe to rope, but I never did go."

Tío told me that every year after the Madison Square Garden rodeo they moved on to the Boston Garden for the last rodeo of the tour. One year a grudge match developed between Toots Mansfield and Clyde Burk. Toots won in Boston, but Clyde kept on saying that he could beat him, and would beat him like a drum if he gave him a chance. After a couple of days of chiding, they decided to move closer to home, and have a six-calf match in Midland, Texas. After the Boston Garden rodeo was over a caravan traveled to Midland, Texas. They drove without stopping. In the Salinases car, one of about ten cars in the caravan, it was Tío, Toots, and Tony. Each would drive as long as a tank of gasoline lasted, then at the fill-up, another would take over. Long distance phone calls let the Texas crowd know that the match was on and the contestants on their way. Rodeo people, promoters, bettors, and stock contractors became involved.

Once in Midland, the betting started. Roy Adams, a gambling man from Arizona, and Hal Ramsey, another bettor, were backing Clyde Burk against Toots Mansfield. Ernest Lane from Odem heard about the match and made it up from Corpus Christi. They got together for a meal, and to talk about the match roping. The morning of the match, Ernest came around to visit Tío and told him that he had bet $10,000 on Toots, did Tío want any part of the bet. Tío took $5,000 of the bet—he knew what he had with Toots, and Toots would be roping off Tío's horse, Honey Boy.

After several hours, Toots won the match. Then the Burk people wanted a chance to get some of their money back so they challenged Tío Juan to rope a six-calf match against Bob Crosby from New Mexico. Tío checked with Toots and asked him how he thought Honey Boy had fared in the first match, and Toots told him that Honey Boy still had plenty left in him. Honey Boy was not tired. Based on this Tío took the challenge and agreed to the match. Just as he was warming up for the match, Ernest Lane walked up and

In action

told Tío that he had bet $10,000 on Tío, and asked if Tío wanted part of the bet. Tío felt very comfortable after winning $5,000 on Toots's match, and did not want to risk any money, but felt sure that if he were to lose against Bob Crosby without covering any part of the bet that there would be accusations of a sell-out. Reluctantly he took half of the bet. Tío won the match, and another $5,000. He called it the richest afternoon he ever had in rodeo.

Tío told me a story one evening about an old rodeo star. "This guy was a few years older than me, and had been in rodeo way before I even started. He was a bull rider. We got to be good friends. We met in Nueva Yorka [that is what he called New York in Spanish, although the correct pronunciation is Nueva York] many times; we ate at the same places, and stayed at the same hotel. Well this one year, he got this little waitress and started taking her out, and before long the little girl, she told my wife Bertha that she was really in love with the bull rider. Another week went by, and the little girl she got more and more in love with him. Finally, the rodeo was over, and it was time to move on to the Boston Garden for the last

Juan Salinas at a tourist court

rodeo of the season, and the bull rider he skipped out of town. We saw the waitress one more time, and she was crying and crying about losing the bull rider. Well you see, I knew the bull rider, he was married back home in California. I seen him in Boston, and

I didn't say nothing, and he didn't either. After the Boston rodeo, me and my peoples, we drove home to Encinal. A couple of months later, we were getting ready to start on a new season, and we got news that the bull rider got killed on his ranchito in California. He was riding a bull and the bull knocked him up against a steel post, and he got hurt and died several days later."

8

Anthony Salinas Destined to Be World Champion Calf Roper

Tío Tony Salinas, ten years younger than Tío Juan, married at about the time that Tío Juan started on the national circuit. He married his local sweetheart, Lucille Juvenal, from Encinal. In 1938, they were blessed with a little towhead they named Anthony. I have photos of Anthony on the national tour with his parents and with Tío Juan and Toots. As the years went by, Anthony became the little boy at rodeos who went to the middle of the arena at about halftime, and roped a 5-gallon tin can. It was quite a feat for a four- or five-year-old to rope anything. He roped the can, the public loved it, and then he opened the can, and pulled out the winning number of a raffle. Little Tony, or Anthony as we have always called him, grew to be an excellent tie-down calf roper. Having three of the world's greatest calf ropers as coaches—Tío Juan, Tío Tony, and Toots—and the world's best roping horses at his disposal meant that Anthony was sure to become World Champion.

Juan always claimed that Tío Tony was better than he was, Tony being younger, much quicker, and more athletic, but Juan said that his consistency in making the catch separated him from Tony. As they say, a small, young bull will whip a big, old bull any day. Among others, in the early 1940s, Tío Tony won the tie-down roping in Springfield, Missouri, and at Frontier Days in Cheyenne, Wyoming.

Little Tony progressed through the years and was very good. He went to Southwest Texas State College in San Marcos, Texas, and roped on the rodeo team there in the mid-1950s, where he captured

Traveling troupers, 1940. Left to right: Juan Salinas, Tony
Salinas, Anthony Salinas, Lucille Salinas, Toots Mansfield

collegiate honors in rodeo. He was on his way to compete for the
World Championship; however, he picked another of his coaches'
habits instead of rodeo; he acquired a preference for gambling.

Anthony did not pursue rodeo like he could have, and by the
1970s he had become a very successful professional gambler. He
lived in San Antonio, Texas, and rumor was he had the biggest
betting book in Texas—simply stated, he was a bookie. Like everything else he was taught, he did it to the best of his ability, and
he was one of the biggest bookies. He was doing great, but there
was one big problem: gambling was illegal in Texas at the time.
With a few exceptions, it still is. This was a time when bingo, lot-
tery, and liquor by the drink were still against the law in Texas.

Inevitably, Anthony wound up in trouble. The first time, he was
able to get off without much of a problem. The second time, however, he was arrested by the FBI. If you know anything about law
enforcement, you should know that there is a huge difference be-

Little Tony Salinas

tween an arrest by local law enforcement, state law enforcement, and the Feds. When the Feds bust you, you are plain in trouble!

Anthony was in big trouble—he was facing a prison sentence for gambling activity using telephone lines and crossing state lines for illicit purposes. I remember vividly Tía Lucille, his mother, coming to see me at my law office and asking that I write a letter of recommendation to the federal judge, asking for leniency.

She told me things about Anthony that I did not know. From a young age he had always worked very hard at whatever work was available and had made plenty of money. When he was about fifteen he bought his own new car—a black 1951 Mercury. He worked around Encinal. He sold milk from a milk cow he owned. He established a movie theater in tiny Encinal at some time in his youth. He was an active and proactive young man, always trying to make a buck, very ambitious and hardworking. From her history and what I knew about my cousin, who was just a few years older than I was, I wrote a letter to Judge D. W. Suttle, the federal judge in charge of Anthony's case, pleading for mercy. I understand that there were dozens of letters similar to mine.

I don't know whether it was the letters or the fact that Anthony had some of the best lawyers in South Texas, but something worked. The judge sentenced him to five years in the federal penitentiary, but probated the sentence on condition that Anthony move to Las Vegas where gambling was legal. The sentence was so unique and out of the ordinary that it made *Ripley's Believe It or Not*.

In a flash, Anthony was on his way to Las Vegas with his wife, Helen, and young son A. C., and to this day he still lives in Vegas. I understand that Anthony runs one of the largest odds-making outfits in Vegas, and still bets quite a bit. I hear you can look him up simply by asking at any of the large hotels. When Anthony made his move to Vegas, one gambler by the name of Jimmy the Greek was very popular. Shortly thereafter, we saw a tabloid that came from Vegas, featuring my cousin Anthony as Tony the Mex.

One evening after supper Tío Juan and I were sitting in his living room watching TV and talking. He said that one evening when Anthony was settling his business before leaving for Las Vegas, he showed up at Tío's house. He told Tío that he had some money buried at Tío Tony's ranch, and would Tío Juan go with him as a guide. Tío Tony had died a few years earlier, and Anthony had not been to the ranch in many years. Tío said they drove out to the ranch, and approached the gathering pens and the windmill. Anthony got a shovel and a pickax out of the truck, took some visual measurements, and began digging. He dug for about 20 minutes, with no results, and then asked Tío if anything had changed through the years. Did someone move the pens? Did someone move the windmill? Tío Juan allowed that there had been no change in any of the improvements. Anthony kept digging, he dug for about another hour, and then finally he hit the object he was looking for. Tío Juan said it was a small bundle of money wrapped in a black plastic bag. He said Anthony opened it to make sure it was his stash, "it's my savings account, Tío; I need it to get to Las Vegas." It was only two thousand dollars, but obviously enough to make a difference.

In October 1998, the *San Antonio Express-News* ran a rather large feature article on Anthony and his gambling history. At the very end of the article, I was pleased to see that Anthony delivered a fine message to all young people: "Don't get into gambling. You won't make it. Those who oppose gambling are right. Gambling is a disease. I can understand why some people want to outlaw it. I have been blessed with the ability to make gambling work. But most cannot control it." In addition was a message to drug users: "Weak people take drugs. I don't like weak people. Show me someone on drugs, and I'll show you a loser." Although his story may sound romantic and exciting, and I am sure he will never admit it, it has been a roller coaster and very rough road for him.

Because of living with Tío Juan, I know that from the many years of rodeo and cowboying together, and being the only nephew he helped to raise, he loved Anthony and was always glad to hear from him, but he did not like his occupation.

9

World War II Adjustments

The Salinas brothers were rodeo performers, but they were also cattle raisers. The cattle raising got them an exemption from the military draft during World War II. True, they spent a lot of their time traveling around the country roping and having a good time, but back home they were producing beef for the nation.

World War II changed everyone's habits. Rodeo participants were no exception. Gasoline and rubber tires, among other commodities were rationed. The Armed Forces got first pick over the public, the consumer. Rationing stopped people from traveling in the way they were accustomed to. Stamps or tokens were needed to buy gasoline and tires. The war curtailed traveling all over the nation. Juan and Tony could drive to some rodeos within the state of Texas, but they could not travel throughout the nation, and this held true for all cowboys, not just the Salinas brothers.

Nevertheless, as the adage goes, "where there is a will, there is a way." In an article by Art Chapman in the *Fort Worth Star Telegram*, the author explains that for years, in the fall of each year, Everett Colborn, the promoter of the Madison Square Garden Championship Rodeo, produced a huge rodeo in Dublin, Texas. After the Dublin rodeo, all of the rodeo stock animals and cowboys would take a train trip to New York City to the Championship Rodeo at Madison Square Garden. This went on for years. When World War II came around, it was a natural for Tío Juan and Tío Tony to hook up with the rodeo train.

Tío told me that after the Dublin rodeo they were to meet in nearby Stephenville, Texas. That is where everyone boarded the

Tying up

train during the World War II years for the trip to Madison Square Garden. Try to imagine a trainload of cowboys and cowgirls on the train for several days. Tío explained that they boarded the horses in several cars, and the equipment went in a baggage car. They slept in Pullman cars and spent all their spare time in the club cars. He said it was a roaring, railroad party for the duration; they had a ball, and could not wait until next year. After the war, the trip was by car again. I say car, because Tío always preferred a car to a pick-up. It provided more room for riders like Toots and Tony, and more room for luggage. One of today's fully loaded pick-up trucks with four doors, lots and lots of room, and a huge engine would have been great. Nevertheless, Tío always had a new Chevrolet auto.

The same *Fort Worth Star Telegram* article gives an excellent account of the train trips. In an interview with first-time participant Lanham Riley, he explains about the first calf roper he ever saw at the Garden, "his name was Juan Salinas, and I'll never forget it. He was a big man, 6-foot-3 and weighed about 200 pounds. He runs out there and ropes this big blue heifer and he never did get her on the ground. That bell rang at the end of the 65 seconds and

Clowning around at tourist court. Juan Salinas
(left) and Toots Mansfield (right)

she had kicked all his britches off. He wore khaki britches and the material was completely gone on one leg. The people just hooped and hollered."

On one of the Sunday drives I took with Tío Juan, we drove down a country road and passed a sign on a ranch gate, and Tío provided another of his stories. "Those people there, they had one son that was drafted during World War II. They just simple peoples, and they ain't got no schooling. The boy he ain't never even been outta the county. All his life he spent on the ranch, working cattle, chopping wood, and the like. Well he got his draft notice, and they asked around town about it, and they were told that the young man had to go report to San Antonio on a certain day, and then they was gonna take him somewhere for boot camp.

"On the day he was scheduled to go, he got on the train in Encinal, at the old depot, with a bunch of other cowboys from Encinal, and they went on to San Antonio, and from there to Louisiana or some place around there for boot camp. Well the other boys from Encinal, when they got back from the war about a year, year and a half later, they told us the story that this boy he kinda went into shock when he got to Louisiana. He got very homesick, and wouldn't talk to nobody, and wouldn't do the drills, just lay in his bed like a baby all curled up, and about a month later he just died. They say he died of a broken heart, or died from homesickness, or just plumb give up. Isn't that strange? Huh?"

10

After Ten Years, The Party's Over

Time eventually takes care of everything, they say. With athletes, time means that eventually the aging process takes over and the body starts to wear out, and consequently slow down. It is a message that it is time to take it easy or quit. I know now that Tío Juan's body did not quit on him until he was about eighty-five years of age, ten years before his death. However, I am sure that it did slow down. Therefore, at age forty-five, the cowboy had to call it quits. He could not win anymore, he was too slow, he knew it, and regretfully, he decided to quit making the trip around the nation. He decided it was time to stay home and work.

Although at age forty-five he was too old to compete with the young lions on the Rodeo Cowboys Association circuit, he was still good enough to win the local ropings, even against the young men. He won many ropings for the next ten to twelve years. The betting continued, and he continued to make money. From reviewing his and Tía Bertha's photo collection, I can safely say that his last roping was in 1966.

Tío Juan kept roping around the South Texas area. Mostly he was invited to match and jackpot ropings. As the years went by, most of his appearances were at old men's ropings, also called old timers' ropings.

Once, Tom East called and told him that there was a roping in Hebbronville, Texas, and they wanted Tío Juan to match rope against Tom East. A friend of theirs, whose name shall remain

Bertha and Juan, ca. 1950

unknown, was promoting the roping. The deal was that Tom, Juan, and the promoter would split the profits three ways. Tío agreed, and at the set date showed up with his horses and gear. Tío beat Tom on six calves, and then roped two more calves for good measure. After the roping, they hung around waiting for the promoter to tally up the gate, the concessions, and all other payments, and

as we say in Spanish, *partir la sandia*, split the watermelon. After
the promoter finished his bookkeeping he told Tom and Tío that
he had to pay his relative for this, and his other relative for that,
and the other relative for that, so that all the income had been used
on expenses for him and his family, there were no profits. Tío just
looked at the guy, shook his head, and loaded up and headed for
home. Before he left, Tom asked Tío over to his ranch for supper.
As they talked and laughed about how they had been taken, Tom
jokingly told Tío that he felt bad for Tío: "I can get even, I'll steal
a cow from him and get even, but you're gonna be up there in Encinal and too far to get even on your own." They laughed about it.
Of course, Tom never stole a cow from anybody.

Back to ranching in earnest, Tío Juan slowly built up the acreage
that he had for his cattle operation. He rented as much property
as he could find. Very few people knew how big his operation was,
because he considered his cattle business extremely private. Woe
to the fool who asked him how many cows he had and how many
acres he ran, because he would just outright tell him, "That is my
business, and don't ask me again how many cows I got, nor how
many acres I run. I don't ask you how much money you got in the
bank, do I?" It was one of his pet peeves.

In reality, at his peak he probably had about thirty to forty
thousand acres, and ran about 2,000 head of cattle. Numbers vary
constantly in any cattle operation. The weather, the landlords, and
the market are all factors that cause variations. Tío leased about
15,000 acres from the Alexander banking family from Laredo National Bank for decades. The ranch was northeast of Encinal, and
named the Charles Ranch. It was a very remote ranch, hard to get
to, especially in wet weather, but Tío ran cattle on it for years. He
would go in annually and pay the rent to Mr. Maurice Alexander
at the bank. They would usually sit for an hour or so to talk about
ranching and cattle. Maurice is the only landlord I know of who
reduced the rent when the cattle economy was bad. Maurice grew
up on the family ranches around Laredo, rode his horses at least
weekly to check on his cattle, and knew the life of the cowboy and
of the cattleman, and when the cattle market went to hell in a hand

basket, he cut the rent. Juan and Maurice enjoyed each other's company and friendship for years and years.

I asked Tío what, in his long life, were the inventions or innovations that he thought were the greatest. I was certain he would say man's trip to the moon, or the invention of the automobile, or the invention of the jet airliner, or something similar. He answered quickly, apparently having made his decision long before I posed the question. "PVC plastic pipe has to be the greatest thing. You just cut the pipe with a hacksaw, and glue it together, and there are all the other parts just to glue, elbows, and couplers, and the others. For us ranchers, that is just great. Before, we have to go buy an expensive and heavy piece of galvanized pipe, then you gotta cut it with a saw, then you gotta have one of them contraptions to put threads on the pipe, and on, and it just lots of trouble. Then in just a couple of years, the pipe rusts through, especially with most of our salty well water. Most of the time you gotta hire a plumber. Not with PVC.

"The other thing that was just great was the U.S. government's invention of the sterile fly, in the 60s or 70s. Before this, we got this little fly that deposit eggs on the newborn calf's belly button, and those eggs develop into worms, and if you don't put medicine on there the calf gonna die. It can happen with a cut on an adult animal too, and on deer and wildlife. It was a mess; we always have to carry a small bottle of worm medicine. It was dark blue, and once you got it on you, you can't get it off. So, you end up with blue hands and blue chaps, and blue saddlebags, blue markings on your shirt, on your pants, on your boots, everywhere. It was a mess, and it was a lot of work too. You ride up on a wormy calf or cow, and you gotta rope the animals and tie its legs, then you gotta put the medicine on, then turn it loose, and you gotta do this to every animals you find that is wormy, or you lose the animal. One time one of my cowboys had cooties on his head, he shaved his head, and then put worm medicine on his head, and he burned his scalp. He ran for the windmill, and poured water on his head for an hour. It burned for a week. Poor dumb fellow. He got blisters on his scalp. Then the government, it come out with this deal here, and I think this is the way it works, I'm not sure. They drop sterile flies from an airplane, and these sterile flies they breed with regular flies, and the regular flies they think they are breeding with a regular fly, and then there are no more of these type of flies. Without these flies, there are no more worms. Without worms, no more calves die. At first I didn't believe it, but sure enough, pretty soon, we would ride up on these little paper boxes out in the *monte*. These boxes were the ones dropped out of the airplane containing these sterile flies. When they hit the ground, they open and all the flies get out so they go and do what they suppose to. Then we started to see the results. No more fly problems and no more worms. Darndest thing. I still don't understand how it works, but it works.

"Then of course there's buffle grass. That grass has saved us. If it were not for buffle grass most ranchers would have gone broke long ago. We just thought we had grass before buffle, but before buffle, we didn't have no grass. It was mostly bare, and every once in while a little carpet of grass. With buffle it is everywhere, we even got trouble keeping it off our lawn. It is everywhere, it lasts through the drought, and just bounces back; it is good. And, I gotta mention air condition. This cool air is great. Before then we was like lizards hiding under whatever shade we can find. It was a very hard life before air condition."

When Juan retired from the PRCA circuit, he probably had about a dozen trophy saddles that he had won at rodeos and ropings. Born and raised during hard times, Juan was not one to put his trophies away. He used all of his saddles in his cattle operation, and slowly wore them out. I presently own six of his trophy saddles, which are all that remain. Most of these are saddles he won in the 1950s. The older saddles that he won in the 1930s and 40s show much use. In 1977, burglars broke into his tack room and stole about five of the best saddles he had. Although I put out feelers trying to recover them, we never saw them again. Of the ones that I have, two are by Shirley Brown from San Antonio, and are engraved Old Mans Roping, Encinal, Texas, 1956 and 1957. Shirley Brown was one of the foremost saddle makers in the state of Texas back then. Obviously, Tío won two of his own charity ropings. Another one is from Rocksprings, Texas, dated 1944. The maker's logo imprint says Mayes Brothers, Del Rio, Texas, Red River Saddle Maker. Another has no engraving or other marking left, it is completely worn smooth. One has engravings showing it is from the Horshoe Inn, Corpus Christi, Texas, made by Kincaid Saddle Shop, and has Old Timers Champion, 1956, Calf Roper engraved on the side. The last one has Juan Salinas engraved on the cantle, all other markings have been worn smooth. The only other leather item I have is a breast collar with large capital letters across it, Halletsville. Perhaps it belonged with a trophy saddle, or maybe he just won the breast collar.

I don't know the ropings that Tío Juan won during his long career, and I doubt a record exists that would help me find out. Consequently, we will never know what prizes he won. Aside from the trophy saddles that I own, I know he won the roping in Phoenix, in 1938, because I have the photo, a buckle, and a silver pocket watch, and the photo shows that he also won a saddle. I have never seen the saddle; it was probably one that had been stolen. The buckle is not like today's 5- and 6-inch gold inlaid monsters. This buckle and the buckle he won in Port Arthur in 1935, are 1 1/2 inches by 3 inches, and very simple by comparison. The Phoenix buckle is sterling, and reads, "Champion Calf Tier, Prescott Frontier Days, 1938, Presented to Juan Salinas by N. Porter Co. Phoenix, Ariz." The other reads, "Port Arthur Championship Rodeo, Calf Tie Down Winner, Juan Salinas 1935." It is made of iron. I also have a fine looking 2-quart silver pitcher with the following cryptic message engraved on it.

JH7 TROPHY,
WON BY JUAN SALINAS OF BRANDING SQUAD,
AT THE 19TH ANNUAL RODEO, BARKER, TEXAS, 1938.

I looked up Barker, Texas, on a Texas highway map because I had never heard of it, and could not find it. Upon further search, I found it. It is about an hour west of downtown Houston on Interstate 10, and is now a part of Houston.

I know he won in Burwell, Nebraska, but I have never seen a prize for winning there.

By the time he retired from professional rodeo, Juan and Bertha had built a house in Encinal. They lived in that house for about twenty years. Tío Juan drove the 3 miles to the Salinas Ranch every day. He wanted to see Mamá Minnie, who was now alone at the big house and assisted only by a couple of sharecroppers. All ranching activities for the day began at the home ranch. Granny died in 1943, and rests at the cemetery in Encinal. Her tombstone states that she was born in 1848. Uncle Zack left for Zapata County in the early 1940s. Momma and Tía Maggie married and lived in Laredo. During my early visits to Mamá Minnie's house, Tío Tony and Tía Lucille lived at the ranch. In later visits, I learned they too had a house in Encinal.

I remember spending summers with Mamá Minnie in the old wooden, Victorian-type house. I still have vivid memories of my stays. There was no indoor plumbing, we used the outhouse for our necessities, and we had to draw water from the cistern in a bucket. Mamá Minnie sent us to fetch water, we would take a bucket and cheesecloth, put the cloth over the bucket, use the well bucket to draw water then filter the water into the house bucket through the cheesecloth. That cistern exists today. Because water was limited, bathing was discouraged. The first few years there was no electricity. Lighting was by kerosene lantern.

To everybody in the family Tío Juan was the hero, the rodeo star who went out and made it big. Hero worship is the best way to describe the way the younger generation felt about him. There was something magic about him, something charismatic. We loved to be around him, talk to him, and ask him questions. Although he never had children, he did not mind us; he treated us well, and frequently would bring us snacks and goodies from Encinal. While our visit was to get to know Grandma better, and to experience ranch life, if only for a couple of weeks, our days passed waiting for the Champ. If we were lucky, we saw the men practice roping at the arena. Inexplicably, we could not ride the horses, much less learn to rope. We were city boys, and horses and cattle were dangerous. Truly, we were behind the curve and it would have taken a long time to learn.

Grandma's house was interesting, very different. During the first years, because there was no electricity, cooking was on a wood stove. To this day, when I smell kerosene I crave flour tortillas, re-fried beans, and, get this—French-fried sweet potatoes, and choc-olate milk. These are a part of my mind, forever hand in hand. By the late 1940s Grandma had electric power. I vividly remember eat-ing supper at about five o'clock in the afternoon, looking through the window toward U.S. Highway 81 (later to become Interstate 35) and the railroad track about 200 yards away, and seeing and hearing the black locomotive climbing the rise on its way to San Antonio. I still remember the black engine, the whistle, black smoke, and the chugging sound of the locomotive. The train came and went once a day or every other day. Today, with the North American Free Trade Agreement (NAFTA) not yet at its peak, trains go by about every 30 minutes, 24 hours a day, with a slight pause on Christmas day. By law, the trains must sound a loud whistle at each intersec-tion with a ranch road. Consequently, we can hear it coming and going miles away. The whistle causes our dogs to howl, adding to the din. Auto and truck traffic was about one car every hour or two back then, now it is a car or two every 30 seconds, day and night.

Grandma loved her big house. I also remember vividly that af-ter work hours, she listened to the radio talk shows and the news. These were the days before television. One night she told my cousin Ricky Rubio and me that President Truman was going to speak to the nation on the radio, and she wanted us to go to bed, be quiet, to sleep, and not bother her. We went to bed in the southeast bed-room, each on a twin bed. We were very quiet in the dark, and could hear President Truman speak. I don't remember what he was talking about, but it was probably about trouble in Korea. I kept trying to go to sleep in the dark, when suddenly there was Ricky's growling face right next to mine. He had crawled out of his bed, then on the floor so I could not see him, until he sprang on me. I screamed for help, and Grandma charged in with a leather quirt, gave each one of us a swipe or two, and told us to be quiet. We were very quiet for the next few minutes and then fell sleep.

If we were not outside with the Champ or Tío Tony, one of our pastimes inside the house was using the stereoscope, with a multitude of post cards from around the world. Juan and Tony had brought two for Mamá Minnie from New York City, with hundreds of cards. Some of the cards were domestic, others were from Europe, and curiously, some of the cards were of Tío Juan and Tío Tony roping at the several rodeos where they had performed. The stereoscope is a binocular-type contraption that you look through, hold with one hand, and place double postcards on the far end of the carriage to view the subject of the card in three dimensions.

11

Settling a Score at the Salinas Ranch

After he had been home several years, Tío Juan started his own ropings and rodeos at the Salinas Ranch. He told me that he had three ropings per year—one to benefit the Encinal Lion's Club, one to benefit Immaculate Heart of Mary Catholic Church in Encinal, and one for his own benefit. The ropings at the Salinas Ranch were quite amazing affairs. Tía Bertha always called to invite us to come from Laredo to each of them. The more attendees, the more benefit for whomever. My Dad and Mom drove us from Laredo. It was great to come back to Grandma's ranch and to see the horses and the cowboys. The smell of the barn and of the tack room in particular sent us dreaming of the "old west." We did not get out to the ranch often, so for us kids it was great. The big wooden barn, its smell of leather and horse sweat, made me feel like I was in another world. These were the smells of Grandma's ranch. The arena is about 200 yards southeast of the main house.

A roping was a chance to get back to the "old west," and a chance to see our favorite cowboys, Tío Juan and Tío Tony. The events started at about ten in the morning. We drove past the old wooden barn, paid admission at the gate, and then drove the couple of blocks to the arena. This was the same arena where Juan, Tony, and Toots had practiced years earlier before going on the national tour. By that time the arena had celebrity, just as did the Salinas brothers and Toots. Rodeo fans drove from Laredo, Encinal, Cotulla, Hebbronville, Alice, San Diego, Zapata, and other area towns. Attendance was typically about 1,000. There were no bleachers.

All the cars parked at right angles around the arena fence. The cars that did not fit around the arena parked along the quarter horse racetrack, and the rest simply parked wherever they could find space. There was a 20-acre area of activity and automobiles in Grandma's back yard. There we sat on the car fenders, or on the ground in front of the car, or in the car. Those who had pick-ups backed them up to the fence and sat in the back, or on top of the cab. For a couple of hours we watched the twenty or so ropers ride around flexing their horses, and practicing getting into the box, and generally just warming up. Tío told me that he wrote all his old roping buddies and invited them to the benefit roping, and most accepted. Tío bought a roping saddle from Shirley Brown in San Antonio, known to make the finest saddles in this part of the country. When the cowboys arrived, they pitched in for their pro-portionate share of the cost of the saddle. They each knew there was no jackpot, and that their contribution went to charity. Later Tío said he changed to Tex Tan saddles, because they would give him a big discount and throw in the engraving for free, knowing that the roping was for a charitable purpose. Typically it read, "OLD MEN'S ROPING ENCINAL, TEXAS 1957, or similar words."

By eleven o'clock they started serving barbeque plates at the concession stand—great barbeque meat with pickles, onions, beans, potatoes, and white bread. Then about one o'clock, we could watch about three or four quarter horse races. Tío Juan had built a metal gate for the horses to spring from north of the arena, and they ran toward the concession stand. Again, fans would line the quarter-mile straightaway in their cars, or they would just stand and watch. A loud pistol shot meant the race was on, and then the steeds flashed by in a few seconds.

After the races, the roping began. The roping went on for about 4 hours. At halftime, a young cowboy, six to ten years old, walked to the middle of the arena accompanied by a cowboy. The cow-boy placed a 5-gallon tin rope can in the middle of the dirt. The young boy distanced himself, and then roped the can. The crowd applauded, and then the boy drew out the one or two prizewinners of previously sold raffle tickets.

After the raffle, the next feature was the breakaway roping for the area cowhands. These cowboys made their living roping and working cattle; these were the backbone of the cattle industry, poor guys who worked for a meager wage for the privilege of being in the fine profession of cowboy. These guys would have given whatever they owned to be in rodeo, but simply did not have the talent, the money, or the time. This did not discourage them from competing in the breakaway. This was their time in the spotlight.

Instead of tying the rope to the saddle as in tie-down roping, a piece of string secures the end of the rope to the saddle horn. When the cowboy and horse come out and rope the calf, the cowboy does not have to dismount and tie the calf, all he has to do is stop the horse abruptly, and the roped calf runs off with the rope; when the rope tightens the string breaks. Breaking the string stops the time clock, and the cowboy with the best time wins a prize. Since most of the cowboys drank quite a few beers before their time in the arena, the event was usually very amusing, with cowboys clowning around, and falling all over the horse, or roping the calf and never breaking the string. By this time in the afternoon, most participants did not care whether they won or not.

After the intermission events, the roping continued for another 2 hours, until sunset. Then the announcer named the winners, it was over, and we drove back to Laredo to attend to homework and preparation for Monday.

A week before the very first roping at the Salinas Ranch, in 1949, at a cafe in Freer, Texas, 50 miles east of Encinal, a rowdy cowboy slapped and whipped a waitress for no justifiable reason. The girl was quite upset, and when she went home that evening told her brother, another cowboy. The brother was extremely upset that someone would take advantage of his sister and actually abuse her physically. He steamed for a couple of days. On Wednesday he heard that the rowdy cowboy was going to the races and rodeo at the Salinas Ranch the following Sunday. He inquired to confirm what he had heard, and all who knew told him that the rowdy cowboy would be at the Salinas Ranch. Bent on revenge, the brother asked around to find out who knew what the rowdy cowboy looked like, and would they go with him to the Salinas Ranch on Sunday. There was a volunteer, Alejandro Narvais, ironically a cowboy who worked at the Lincoln Ranch, formerly the Las Blancas Ranch, the Salinas Ranch before it moved to Encinal. On Sunday, the pair drove the 50 miles west from Freer to Encinal and made it to the Juan Salinas Ranch.

After they ate lunch, the brother asked if the rowdy cowboy was around; Alejandro told him that he was sitting on top of a jeep apparently waiting for the running of a horse race. At this point the brother got in his pick-up, drove to about 20 yards behind the rowdy cowboy, pulled out an open sights lever action .30–30 rifle, knelt down on one knee, took aim, and shot the rowdy cowboy in the back right between the shoulder blades.

I heard the shot and ran over to the racetrack. By the time I got there, they would not let kids come around to see what had happened. The news spread like wildfire, we knew that someone had just been killed. You can imagine the excitement for us—first, a chance to go out to the "old west" with horses, and calves, and real honest-to-goodness cowboys, and now a shooting and a murder. I was excited for days. It was horrible and unfortunate for the dead man and his family, but for the young seven-year-old, it is a memory that has lasted through the years.

Tío told me that he was at the horse race gates when he heard the shot. He saw people running all over the place, so came to investigate. When he got to the scene a cowboy from Encinal, Vicente Arce, had grabbed the shooter with both arms, to stop any further shooting. A Webb County deputy sheriff was in the crowd and arrested and cuffed the man. Tío was waiting at the gate when the Webb County sheriff drove out with the killer in hand cuffs. The killer asked that the car stop, and he talked to Tío.

"Did I kill him, Juan?" He asked.

"Yeah, you killed the hell outta him, bullet came right out of his chest," Juan answered.

"Good, that is exactly what I wanted to do," was the retort.

I can imagine that in today's world, a lawsuit would be filed on Monday morning against Tío Juan, for not having security guards, and for not having metal detectors at the admission gate, or for some such reason.

This was not a typical afternoon. In all the ropings at the Salinas Ranch, that was the only instance of violence.

12

Leading a Cattleman's Life

Leaving the circuit meant that Juan and Bertha were home with no travel obligations. Juan and Bertha never had children, and this had freed Bertha to go with Juan to all the rodeos. They enjoyed each other's company, spent countless hours together, and had a good time. I can safely say that they had a great life together. Oh, I am sure they had their ups and downs just like everyone else, but they traveled a lot, they partied a lot. To my knowledge, Tío never had financial difficulties.

When they came home to stay, they exhibited nothing but a wholesome attitude and continued having a good time. They rekindled friendships in Laredo, Encinal, Cotulla, and Beaumont, Tía Bertha's hometown. Bertha had a bridge party every Sunday, her lady friends came over to have lunch and play cards. Periodically the couple went out for dinner with friends such as Bill and Alice Hall, Dan and Musty Sanchez, Oscar and Elsa Laurel, Bill and Irene Stokes, Bob and Polly Coquat, and others from the area. Tony and Lucille Salinas also formed a great part of their social circle. Many times, they had people over to their house for a party. Occasionally, Mucia, my mom, and my dad Abe Palacios, and Tía Maggie and her husband Henry Rubio joined the festivities. I remember coming to one of these parties in 1964 for Tío Juan's birthday. I was twenty-one years old, and felt out of place with all the older folks around. Everyone had a marvelous time.

Tío once told me how he felt about parties. "Well them parties, they Bertha's idea, they're all her idea—she don't got no kids, and

Night out in Mexico. Left to right: Bertha Salinas,
Juan Salinas, Polly Coquat, Bob Coquat

she gets lonely, so she has all these parties. It's getting to where my
cowboy, Manos Pintas, he says my name is not Juan Salinas anymore, it's Juan Parties. Anyhow, I enjoy them, but after I eat, I'm
ready to go on and work. In my opinion, *a los tres dias, la visita y los
muertos apestan*: after three days company and the dead stink."

Very special friends for Juan and Bertha were Robert "Bob" Coquat and his wife Pauline, whom everyone called Polly. Since I did
not become part of Juan and Bertha's life until the 1980s, I am not
privy to details about their early life, other than what Juan has told
me. For example, I really cannot say when the friendship with the
Coquats developed, but it was probably somewhere in the 1950s.
I know Bob was La Salle County Judge sometime in the 1970s.
Bob owned a large ranch about 12 miles northeast of Encinal. He
and Polly lived there and ran a large cattle operation. They had a
very large house, and they too hosted many parties. Polly's sister,
Jane, was married to John Justin of the Justin Boot Company, and
they came to Juan and Bertha's often. I remember that Thanksgiving was a special weekend at the Salinas residence, and about a
dozen visitors from around the state came to partake in the fes-

tivities—the Justins, Ruth and Jigger Alexander, the Pat Welders, Bertha's niece Dee Dee and her husband Louis from Beaumont, Bertha's sister Clara Day and her husband Tommy, Red and Dorris Garret from Port Aransas, and of course, Bob and Polly and Tony and Lucille. I feel that Bob and Polly brought out the best in Tío. If it had not been for them, I think Tío would have just withered away as a cloistered cowboy, and that would have been bad for him, and horrible for Tía Bertha. As it was, Bob and Polly helped them have a good time and make the best of it. On many occasions Bob and Polly took Tío Juan and Tía Bertha to the University of Texas Longhorn football games. Both Bob and Polly were alumni of the University of Texas. On one occasion, both Tío and Bob sat on the Longhorn bench at the special invitation of Coach Darrel Royal.

Charitable work also became a part of their lifestyle after the rodeo circuit. The Laredo Lions Club came to Encinal to form a club, and they enlisted Juan and Tony's help. Lions Club developed a friendship for life between Tío Juan and Joe Puig from Laredo. Joe was a Lion from an early age, and he was very instrumental in installing the club in Encinal. As a result, he got to know and work with Juan, and they were good friends thereafter. I will never forget seeing Joe Puig at Tía Bertha's wake. The body had only been out about 5 minutes, and in comes Joe and his wife. Joe had suffered a stroke, and was having a hard time making an appearance, but he was there for his good friend and fellow Lion.

The Lions Club became very active in Encinal. The club had several fundraisers during the year, including the one roping at the Salinas Ranch. They were able to get streetlights for the city of Encinal. Because Encinal is not a large community, with a population always hovering around 500, putting in streetlights was no small task. Through the years, they were able to raise enough funds to build a small cinder block building for their meetings. It is about a thousand square feet, is at the corner of Tejas and Santa Fe in Encinal, and today stands as the City Hall. Years later, the Encinal Lions Club went into inactivity and the clubhouse just sat there. Through the efforts of the late Dan Sanchez, the Lions Club was going to donate the property to the adjacent Immaculate Heart of Mary Catholic Church, but a former good Catholic, and wife of a deceased Lion, decided that the gift to the church would be improper, raised hell, and the city of Encinal got the building instead. No matter, it went for a good use.

Immaculate Heart of Mary Catholic Church was also a beneficiary of the Salinases benevolence. There was one Salinas Ranch roping per year for it. Monsignor E. G. Bartosch, who was the parish priest when I moved to Encinal in 1982, told me that about once a year at one of the Salinases parties, just when everyone was feeling in a good mood, Tía Bertha would go around and solicit a calf from every rancher in the room. Before the night was over, she might have ten or more calves, to be gathered, sold, and the proceeds given to the church. In 1955, hurricane remnant winds leveled the frame church building that stood on wooden stilts. This signaled the need for a new church building. Tío Juan and Tía Bertha did their share in contributing to the new concrete block building. It is the building presently in use as the church.

In the late 1960s, Bob Coquat suggested to Tío that he run a couple of youth ropings per year. These would be occasions to teach the youngsters how to rope calves, or to allow beginners to hone their skills. Juan and Bertha agreed and held many of these ropings. I know many area cowboys and ropers, now adults, who remember the days at the Salinas arena where they roped in public for the first time and learned from all the coaches surrounding them. Youngsters from the area with roping aspirations came to rope in competition with others similarly situated.

Juan and Bertha lived in Encinal after their return from the circuit, but almost immediately began making plans for the return to the Salinas Ranch. They planned to raze the old wooden, Victorian-style house and build a new residence, at the exact same location as the wooden structure. Mamá Minnie died in 1951, so the wooden house sat vacant for many years. I remember about 1959 going to the old house with Momma and Tía Maggie to sift through Mamá Minnie's belongings for collectibles. It was the last chance, because the house would be gone soon.

In 1963, Juan and Bertha began work on the new house. It was a modern concrete-floor and cinder-block-wall building, with air conditioning and beautiful paneled walls and ceilings. The only thing preserved from the old house, as a memento from the past, was the cistern, and a water-well decoration and arch of bricks around the opening. The cistern stands today as a memorial to the cistern built almost one hundred years ago.

The first room in the house that one came to from the back was the den. On the walls in the den were a dozen or so photographs from Tío Juan's adventures on the rodeo circuit. There were panoramic photos of Frontier days in Cheyenne, in 1937; Cotulla, Texas, Cowboy Christmas, July 4, 1933; Burwell, Nebraska, 1938; San Francisco, California, World's Fair, 1939; Southwestern Livestock Show and Rodeo in Forth Worth, 1938; and four shots of either the basement in Madison Square Garden or City Hall in New York City at the World Championship Rodeo, for 1943, 1945, and 1946, Juan's last year on the circuit. There were also photos of Tío Juan when he won the roping in Phoenix in 1938, of Tío and Tía with Roy Rogers at the Cowboys Turtle Association banquet, and other similar photos. Looking closely at the photos you could see Buffalo Bill Cody, Gene Autry, Roy Rogers, and of course, Juan Salinas and Tony Salinas. Walking into the den, you felt like you were in a cowboy history museum.

Tío said that one of the nicest and most cordial of all the cowboys was Gene Autry. "Old Gene Autry, he said hello to me every time I seen him. In 1939, we got to Salinas, California, one day early. In Salinas, California, they had this deal that if anyone rode a horse in the rodeo parade they would get a free pass to the rodeo. So there were dozens and dozens of peoples on horseback in the parade and they don't need us rodeo people to be in the parade. So, we was watching the parade, and Gene Autry was the parade marshal. I could see him coming up the street a ways off. Then he come right up to where we was standing, and he turned and saw us, and he brought his horse right over to where we were, he dismounted, came on over to us and shook hands, and hugged the womens, and said he was real happy to see us at the rodeo, chatted for a couple of minutes, then got on his horse Champion and caught up with the head of the parade. Real nice guy. You probably don't know but he wrote that song about the deer with the red nose, and he made a bunch of money with that song. Course he made movies and all, and even owned a baseball team in California, and made lots of money there too."

Discussing the move back to the ranch, and building a new house, Tío Juan made the following comment one evening: "I can't understand womens. When we lived at the ranch, Bertha couldn't stop saying 'let's move into town,' then we moved into town, and then it was 'let's move out to the ranch.' When we lived on the ranch, it was 'be sure and bring water from town, 'cause I don't like this rain water.' When we moved into town, it was, 'please bring me some rainwater, 'cause it's the best water there is.' I never understand womens."

We sat in the den one evening and Tío related the following story: "I rodeoed with Reba McIntire's grandfather, and later her father was in rodeo too. Anyways, one day Reba and her dad Clark showed up here at the house, they was here selling or buying horses or bulls, I don't remember what. They came in and stayed quite a while, that young lady she sat right there on the living room rug, and sang up a storm. Her daddy asked her to sing for us and she did, just sat right in the middle and sang." I remember Mr. Clark McIntire, Reba's father, when we took Tío to the induction ceremony at the National Cowboy Hall of Fame in 1991. He was the first person we met and greeted. He remembered Tío well, and Tío recognized him.

On occasion, Tío and Tía had parties that included horseback riding. These were primarily with the Coquats. Sometimes for the rodeos, everybody wanted to ride horses. It was time to get Tía Bertha's gentle horse, and time for one of the longest-lasting jokes around the Salinas Ranch. Tía did not need a powerful workhorse, but instead needed a tired, old, gentle horse that would not buck her off, or take off running at a hundred miles an hour; she needed a horse she could handle without much effort. Tío Juan looked around and found a ten-year-old gelding that had seen better days. He was pot bellied and swayed back, and could care less about bucking and running a sprint.

Salinas Ranch, 1970. Courtesy Al Rubio, Austin, Texas

Tío named him Fundillo, or Butt. Tío waited until the crowd gathered then hollered out at the ranch hand, *"Anda agárrale el fundillo a Berta"* ("go grab Bertha's butt"). Meaning to go get her horse, of course. Everybody laughed and laughed about it, and every time it was just as if it were a fresh, new joke. Everyone stood around waiting for Tío Juan to yell out the order, *"Anda agárrale el fundillo a Berta."*

13

A Real True Friend

When Juan was growing up at *La Becerra*, he made friends with all the kids his age in the area. While on the rodeo circuit, Tío drifted away from his local friends. When he returned, he was married and had formed a different social circle. As Tío got older, he slowly came back to his early friendships. Tío Tony died in 1973; Bob Coquat died shortly thereafter. Dan Sanchez died in the 1980s, and so it went. Little did anyone know that Juan, the oldest, would outlive them all.

One of the old friendships that solidified in the later years was that with Ramon Flores. Ramon was born on a ranch around the Encinal area. I became well acquainted with him during the last ten years of his life. He told me that as a child his family was very poor. He remembered running around in bare feet for most of his early years. Imagine walking barefoot around a 10-mile perimeter. He told me it was common. His early years helped him gain a healthy love for farming. He was a farmer at heart, and could make crops grow as if by magic. Another of the loves of his life was dancing. He said he would go to the occasional Saturday night dance, barefoot, with only a dime in his pocket. Because the admission was a quarter, he had to wait for a couple of hours before they would take his dime and let him in to dance.

As a young man, Ramon married Ramona Campos. She inherited a small tract of land, just north of the Salinas Ranch. They formed their homestead on this tract. Ramon related how life was so hard during the 1920s and 30s. He said he cleared land of brush and trees by hand with an ax and pickax for $3 per acre. One of the luckiest things that happened to Ramon, aside from marrying Ramona, was getting a job on a road crew with the Southern Pacific Railroad. This job, and the union wages and benefits that came with it, allowed him to live comfortably. He built a nice house and was able to buy more land from his in-laws. He was able to get into the farming business in earnest, and most importantly, he was able to provide those of his children who wanted it a college education. His daughter Tonia did not go to college, but her husband Jorge Adams was able to get a job with the railroad. Their two sons, J. J. and Cesar, work for the successor railroad, Union Pacific, to this day. Ramon's sons Margarito and Miguel both went to Southwest Texas State College and earned their degrees and teaching certificates. Margarito became principal of the Encinal Elementary School and is now semiretired; he also followed his father's footsteps as a farmer. Margarito's son Larry is a premed student on a scholarship at St. Mary's University, San Antonio. His son Juan did not attend college but became supervisor of the print shop at the University of Texas at San Antonio. He has now retired to the Flores Ranch.

Ramon Flores claimed to be illiterate, and to speak only Spanish. I believe, however, that he could understand every word of English he heard, and though he might have been illiterate, he was an extremely intelligent man. He was very gentle, and I could talk to him for hours. He told me all the old stories of our family, and his family, and about Encinal and the area. I gradually gained a love for the man. He was a good father, hard worker, and religious man. I marveled at how a supposedly illiterate man had witnessed the revelation of God, and become a faithful Christian. He lived and worked outdoors all his life; it is not hard to understand how he came to this revelation and belief.

By the time I got to know Ramon he was already retired from the railroad, or as they say in Encinal, *el camino de fierro* (the iron road). He farmed and raised cattle, always managing to come up with a crop of hay, or watermelons, or oranges, when no one else could. Ramon was a very likeable person, many of his friends called him Moncito, short for Ramoncito. The *ito* is always added in Spanish to describe something small or tiny, or to make the term or word one of endearment.

Both being semiretired, Tío Juan and Ramon migrated toward each other, and helped each other every way possible. The routine was simple—they met at Ramon's house about seven in the morning, then they raced into Encinal to the Reyes Cafe and had coffee and a roll or a breakfast taco. They would take their sweet time and reminisce about everything under the sun. Then they would go to the post office, and possibly cuss out the postmistress for not having the mail up as promised. Then they would go home, Ramon to his house and Juan to his. They would then work on their own until the next morning. Occasionally, they would help each other work cattle, and then they would take the calves to the cattle auction in Cotulla. They attended the sale, ate lunch, waited for their checks, then drove back to Encinal.

If they had gone to a sale and sold calves, the next day they would travel to Laredo, 38 miles south, to the Laredo National Bank, to deposit their checks. There are a couple of funny stories about these trips into Laredo. While Juan was extremely healthy and roped and worked hard until he was about eighty-five, right about that time he began to experience problems with his eyesight. He ended up with very thick glasses, and while it appeared he could drive all around the Encinal area, we began to get complaints from neighbors who warned us that he was driving in the middle of the highway, or on the wrong side, or running people off the road. Because of this eyesight problem, Ramon drove Juan's pick-up into Laredo. Juan had a 1987 Chevrolet pick-up with the new space-age dashboard buttons and dials. Even I had trouble reading the dials and figuring out how to run the air, the radio, and other accessories.

On this one very hot day, Ramon and Juan took off, and could not figure out how to get the cooling system to work. As it turned out the heater was on high and they could not figure out how to turn it off. They drove to Laredo in 10-mile spurts. Every 10 miles they would stop and walk around the truck and cool down. Then they would do it all over again, until they arrived in Laredo, soaking wet from sweat. They drove to the first friend they could find on the north end of Laredo, Frank Leyendecker, at the Exxon distributorship. They went in and got Frank to come out and show them how to turn on the cooling. All had a good laugh.

Another good story is about the time they went to the parking lot of the Laredo National Bank, got out, slammed the car door, and went in to make their calf sale deposits. When they came out, Ramon went to the driver's side, and noticed that he had locked the keys in the truck. They went back into the bank and tried to get someone to call the fire department, and they could not get a response. After about an hour's wait, the security guard decided to go out to the truck with them. When he approached the truck, the guard walked up to the driver's side and looked in. He slowly investigated the entire scene, and then spoke up. "Well gentlemen, I am looking at the truck, and I try the handle and sure enough, it is locked. I look in the truck and sure enough, the key is locked in the truck. However, I look at the window on this door here, and the window is down, so I am going to reach in and open the door from the inside. See. Have a good trip home." The two old men laughed all the way home.

After they left the bank, the next stop was at El Tío Hut restaurant. They always called and asked me to have lunch. I hurried from the office downtown and joined them. It was funny getting the call. In ranch fashion, Tío would say, "Ricardo Palacios, this is Juan Salinas, I want you to come to lunch with me." It wasn't, "this is your uncle," or "this is Tío Juan," but the formal "this is Juan Salinas." We had many memorable meals at the Tío Hut. We talked about everything imaginable. I have always enjoyed listening to older fellows talk. I think back and remember many hours spent talking to elderly people, some known, some unknown, just soaking in all the history and wisdom. The stories they tell are always so interesting. Now, on some occasions, I happen to be the older fellow who tells the stories.

After the meal at the Tío Hut, they would drive to the Cakeland Bakery on Saunders Street and each would buy a bag of *pan dulce*, Mexican pastry, to take home. The next day they would take some of the pan dulce to Reyes Cafe in Encinal for coffee. The owner of the cafe just shook her head—her customers bringing in their own rolls, instead of buying hers. They lived this way the last ten years of their lives.

Ramon was lucky in finding his Ramona. They worked side by side from the time they married until old age and health, or lack thereof, did them apart. Ramon told me that Ramona would work right beside him, whatever he did in the fields, whether picking crops or chopping weeds. He also told me that she could dress a deer or wild hog better than most men. He admired her resourcefulness tremendously. I could tell from talking to Ramon that he and his wife were dearly in love. Naturally, you get this feeling when talking to most married couples, but this was unique. He spoke of a special relationship. Being companions and friends for fifty or so years, raising a family in adverse times, had brought this couple closer together than most. When Ramona died, most people said Ramon was never the same again. He spoke often about her, and about how much he missed her, and about how he felt cheated at not having her around. He was very lonely after her death.

Both Ramon and his wife Ramona were diabetic. In the late 1980s, they asked me to prepare wills for them. In fact, Ramona was already in the hospital. I complied with their wishes and wrote the documents. Unfortunately, a couple of days later Ramona died. A couple of weeks later Ramon contacted me about having the will probated. I prepared the requisite application and other documents and filed same in court. A few weeks after that, we had a court date to go before the probate court judge.

Ramon and I took the elevator to the second story of the courthouse. In the foyer and lobby were about thirty or forty young couples, each young man trying hard not to look at his young woman, and vice versa. Ramon looked curiously at the young people, and asked me what they were doing there. I told him that they were there for their divorces. He was shocked. He almost cried thinking about his Ramona. "If they could only realize how foolish they are being, how I wish my Ramona was here, to love her and help her and be with her, and these young punks can't wait to get rid of each other. They have not even given it a chance." This was a complete disappointment for him.

As the years crept on, Ramon and Juan continued their routine. In 1988, Tía Bertha began to get ill. My ex-wife took her to San Antonio for doctor visits several times. When she could not take her, my cousin Margie would take her, but the trips seemed to be getting more frequent. Finally, in 1990 she took a turn for the worse. The San Antonio doctor ordered that she be taken to Laredo and not San Antonio. There was no longer a need for the long trip to San Antonio. We took her in to the hospital in Laredo. The next day, I wanted to make sure that Tío Juan went to the hospital to see her. Ramon drove him in to Laredo, they called me when they arrived in Laredo, and I told them I would meet them at the hospital. I took them both up to Tía Bertha's room, Ramon and I stood in the background as Juan and Bertha said their last goodbyes. They were so much in love, and felt so bad not to be able to help each other. They talked and chatted as Ramon and I stood quietly in the back of the room. It was a truly sad sight, two old folks realizing that the end is near, probably remembering the fine memories they shared. Finally, Juan said, "I love you Momma, and I got to go back to the ranch." Bertha understood, she said she loved him. Juan was ninety years old; she repeated her declaration of love for him, and told him to be careful. Tía Bertha died two hours later.

Ramon continued to have trouble with diabetes. Ramon told me that as a young man he would go out and kill a wild hog, and carry it back home on his shoulders. He, Ramona, and the kids would skin it out, dress and butcher it, and he would eat half a side of ribs in one sitting. He mentioned this in his frustration of trying to keep to his diet when his diabetes became serious. He told me it was impossible for him. Lettuce and tomato salads were no substitute. I think he tried but it was quite difficult. After Ramona died, the task of caring for him fell to his daughter Tonia. He complained of trying to eat lettuce, tomato, and asparagus, when what he really craved was a side of pork ribs or something similar.

Ramon died in 1992 doing what he loved best, farming. He and his son Margarito cut and baled the hay crop at the Páncho Ni-

eschwietz farm a couple of miles north of Encinal. It was late afternoon, and as Ramon bent over to pick up a square bale of hay,
he collapsed. He had a heart attack and died a few minutes later.
It was a tremendous loss for his family, for Juan, and for me. I still
think of him often. What a fine man. As we say in Spanish—*Dejó
muy buena huella* (he left a very good imprint).

14

Employees, Good and Bad

In his long life Tío Juan had many employees; some good, and some bad; some memorable, some not; some characters, some not. I could write about many that I knew or heard about, but I write here about just a few.

After returning to Encinal permanently, Juan and Bertha lived in the little town of Encinal, not out on the ranch. Since no one ran for the office of La Salle County Constable, Juan took the job. He got calls on Saturdays and Sundays in particular and anytime that there were any problems in Encinal, especially in the saloons.

Juan had an employee by the name of Jose Garcia. He had a common name, but Jose was not a common person. He was a cowboy, a hard worker, extremely intelligent, and very, very helpful to Juan. He was mature beyond his years, and helped not only as a cowboy, but also in motivating and managing the rest of the cowboys. On Saturdays or special holidays, Jose was sure to be found having a good time. Jose was one of our people we typically call *puro indio*. The Mexican Indian blood dominates and is physically apparent. He was probably full blooded; he had a typical barrel chest, short, broad face, and slanted eyes and forehead—the image of an *Azteca* warrior. I met Jose when I was a child on sojourns to the Encinal area with my dad. I became acquainted with him some then, but not well. I met him again when he was in his eighties. I was a puppy lawyer, and he had just gotten married, and wanted me to help him get a divorce. His caregiver talked him into marrying, and it did not work out. He was about eighty and she was thirty-some. I helped him with his problem, and always enjoyed hearing his stories.

This story about him I learned from Tío Juan. One Saturday night about 11 p.m., around 1948, Constable Juan got a call from someone saying that Jose Garcia had been killed at a dance out in the yard at one of the local saloons. Juan hurried over, and sure enough, there in the middle of the dance floor laid Jose's body in a pool of blood. Juan approached and the people around the body cleared and began to talk about what had happened, giving Juan all the details. Juan bent over and touched Jose's neck for a pulse, and there was none. Someone cut Jose's throat with a knife, and there was a gaping bloody wound just below his chin, and literally running from ear to ear. Juan held his limp wrist, and felt for a pulse and there was none. Juan went inside the saloon, borrowed the phone, and called the sheriff in Cotulla, 30 miles away. The reply was that the sheriff and a couple of deputies were already on their way to Encinal.

Juan returned to the dance floor and started asking questions. Before long, he got all the information he needed on what had happened. Juan walked over to the crowd of onlookers, and grabbed the man who had cut Jose and arrested him. He cuffed him and took him to his car and put him in the back seat. After about 20 minutes, the sheriff and deputies from Cotulla arrived. Juan was de-briefed and gave them the details. The sheriff began an investigation to confirm Juan's findings. This was an era before EMS and rural ambulances. The body just lay on the dance floor. Finally, after a couple of hours passed, Jose Garcia's family asked if they could take the body to the funeral home in Laredo. The sheriff asked Juan if there was any reason why they could not take the body, and Juan said there was none as far as he was concerned. So, at about 1 o'clock in the morning, his family took Jose Garcia's body for burial.

Well, as it turned out the family did not take him to the funeral home, they took him to the emergency room at Mercy Hospital in Laredo, where doctors confirmed that Jose was still alive. Jose was in the hospital for several weeks. His vital blood vessels were intact, but his larynx—his voice box—was sliced in two. Years later,

I talked to the elderly man many times. He had a raspy voice to say the least, and had almost no volume, but he was very much alive. We became good friends. When I met him, he was bartender at the *cantinita* in Adamiville, several miles east of Encinal on Highway 44. He worked there for a couple of days then moved into Encinal to stay for a few days and then went back out to the cantina. I visited there a couple of times. Later, he invited me to a party given for him on his birthday out in the *monte* by the Adamis and other friends. He bragged about having to get into the pens and teach the youngsters how to work cattle.

Aside from being constable in Encinal, Tío Juan was also Webb County special deputy sheriff, and that also brought adventures. "My daddy was sheriff of Webb County. All of the old families grouped into the *Partido Viejo* (the Old Party), some called it the Independent Club. We were sometimes asked to help with elections. I was special deputy sheriff for Webb County, and carried a *credencial* all my life. One time in the 1930s, I was called to go to Laredo, because there was some kind of labor problem.

"A labor organizer was trying to call a strike, or a blockade of some sort. The Partido Viejo was determined to stop the demonstration. I showed up in Laredo, went to visit my tías, Tía Chente and Tía Margarita, for a couple of hours. Then I was told to go to the old viaduct over the Tex Mex Railway on Meadow Street. I showed up at about five in the afternoon, and there were about twenty deputies and some strike breakers there. By about six thirty or seven the group had grown to about one hundred special deputies, regular deputies, constables, and hired guns. The leader told us about the labor organizer, and his group, and the demonstration they were planning to blockade the highway to Zapata right there at the Tex Mex viaduct.

"Later that night we saw the headlights coming. There were about ten cars. Everyone braced for the fight. The cars parked about a half a block away, and the labor strikers gathered and talked by their cars. There were about fifty of them.

"About fifteen minutes went by, and the group of laborers walked toward the deputies, led by the labor organizer. Surprisingly, there was no violence. The labor organizer started talking to the deputy sheriff in charge, and they talked and talked for about 30 minutes. They discussed the blockade, and the possibility of a big fight. Little by little, the deputies began to befriend the labor organizer, and they started joking and laughing.

"Two hours later, it was apparent that there would be no violence. The laborers started leaving car by car. Soon only the labor organizer and five men were still there. The labor organizer kept talking to the deputies. After a while, the deputies realized that the crisis was over, they brought out some beer and whiskey. Somebody brought out some boxes, and the group sat around and drank for two or three hours.

"When the labor organizer was drunk and completely softened, the deputies arrested him. They told us to leave, the crisis was over. I got in my car and drove to the tías, and then drove home to Encinal.

"The next day I heard from the newspaper that the deputies had tied the labor organizer to the front of a car, and paraded him all over Laredo stinking drunk and passed out. Then they took the organizer to a warehouse, and then beat him up. They stripped him and started hosing him down with water. One of the hired guns got carried away and inserted a water hose in the labor organizer's behind, and filled him with water. By six in the morning, the labor organizer was dead. I never was called on any duty again.

"One time I was in Laredo and was stopped by a traffic cop. He said I was driving too fast or something like that. As he walked over to me, I pulled out my Webb County special deputy sheriff *credencial* and showed it to him. I said, '*yo también soy achichinque del partido viejo, igual que tú*' ('I am also an Old Party flunky just like you'). The cop didn't like what I said, but he looked at the card and told me to get the hell outta there. I left."

When Papá Antonio was still alive, a ranch hand by the name of Don Leandrito came by the ranch and asked for work. He had worked for another ranch for decades, the ranch was sold, and he had no family, and no place to go, no place to live. Papá Antonio told Tío Juan to hire him, and let him live in one of the storage rooms in the barn. For several years he helped around the ranch with minor chores. After about a year at the Salinas Ranch, Don

Leandrito began telling anyone who would listen that he was preparing for his death, that he did not want to trouble anyone with his passing, and that he had figured out how to make his demise easy and trouble free. He said he would take a shotgun and a gallon of kerosene, go off into the brush, gather firewood, and make a huge bonfire, then shoot himself above the fire, causing imminent cremation, thus disposing of his remains without giving anyone any trouble with his death. Nobody took him seriously about these plans, but he kept repeating them.

One day Tío Juan and Tío Tony were building wooden feed bunkers by the big barn; they saw Don Leandrito leave the barn carrying a shotgun and a gallon can of kerosene. They called out to him and asked him where he was going, but Don Leandrito did not respond. They looked at each other, and decided not to interfere. Several minutes passed and Tío Tony noticed a plume of smoke coming from the brush north of the house. He told Tío Juan about it, and again they decided to ignore the obvious. They kept waiting for the gunshot, and none came. Finally, after about half an hour, they noticed Don Leandrito walking back to the barn. He carried the shotgun, and the kerosene can. When he got near they asked him what had happened, and he replied that *"todavia quiero vivir unos diítas más"* ("I still want to live a few more days"). Juan and Tony laughed, and talked about this for the rest of their lives.

One time I asked Tío if at age ninety-three he felt that he had lived sufficiently and whether he was ready to pass on. His short reply was *"quiero vivir unos diítas más."*

Another of Juan's memorable employees was Francisco Garcia, alias Páncho Manos Pintas (Spotted Hand). My dad, Abe Palacios, dropped out of Laredo High School in 1927 to become a wage-earning cowboy. His father, my grandfather Ignacio Palacios, suffered a cerebral stroke; there was no income at home, so off to work Abe went. His first job was at a cattle ranch in Mexico working for Don Alfredo Matthews who was married to Ethel Welhausen from Encinal. Dad worked there for several years. Dad told me a story of working cattle on the Matthews ranch in the canyons in Coahuila. He was following a trail for about an hour, the trail made a 90-degree turn and suddenly he came upon a young man strung up by his thumbs, apparently badly beaten and left to die. Dad said that he was not able to find out why this had occurred. Dad pulled out his pocketknife, cut the ropes, got off his horse, and gave the young man water from his canteen. After about half an hour the young man came to. Dad told him to wait, went and got help and an extra horse, and took him back to headquarters. The young man recovered, and stayed on as a hand working for *Don* Alfredo. The young man was Páncho "Manos Pintas" Garcia.

Mamá Minnie died in 1951, and each of the children inherited their own share of land to work and enjoy. Mom and Dad decided to try a cattle operation, and the first cowboy we had was Páncho Garcia. Dad found out where he was in Mexico and sent for him. He showed up and went to work immediately. I spent many hours talking to Páncho, and I came to find out that Páncho was born in the United States, but when World War II broke out, he left for Mexico—a draft dodger. He said he had nothing against Hitler, and Hitler didn't even know him, so he saw no reason why he should join the Army and fight. So in coming back to work in Texas, notwithstanding the fact that he was an American citizen, he had to pose as a wetback because he might be arrested for leaving the country during the war. Therefore, he carried fake papers. He got a birth certificate in Encinal from a friend, Alejandro Narvais. Every time he went to Mexico to see his family, he was no longer Páncho Garcia, he was Alejandro Narvais.

Páncho also told me that he had served as a police officer in Nuevo Laredo, and had killed a man in a brawl. Although the homicide was justified, Páncho always feared revenge from the dead man's family. Thus when Páncho went home he felt he had to wear a disguise. He looked a sight. He wore a colorful scarf around his neck, a Hoot Gibson/Hoss Cartwright cowboy hat, and round John Lennon–type sunglasses. Instead of a disguise, he stood out like a red, swollen, sore thumb.

When Mom and Dad tried the cattle business, it became apparent that Dad was not a cattleman and not a businessman. The only thing they got out of the experience was a several-thousand-dollar debt at the bank, which took years to pay off. Upon getting out of the business, Dad asked Tío Juan if he wanted a good cowboy. Good cowboys being hard to find, Tío took Páncho as an employee, and there began a fifteen-year employer-employee relationship that unfortunately ended tragically. Páncho was the type of person who can work best if left alone. He got up at about three in the morning, ate breakfast, and was out in the barn by four, feeding and watering the animals, and ready for the major chore of the day by sunrise. Juan was no slouch when it came to work, so they worked well together. They were together so many hours of the day that they got to where they treated each other like friends, and this meant that they would cuss each other out regularly. By the next day, or in a few hours it was forgotten and over. I can remember watching them work, Juan accusing Páncho of not being worth a plug nickel, and Páncho retorting that Juan was worth less than a plug nickel.

The work schedule was arranged so that Páncho would work for about ninety consecutive days, then take off for thirty. Juan drove him into Laredo, they went to the bank where Páncho cashed his paycheck, and then Juan drove him to the International Bridge, or sometimes even drove him to the train station in Nuevo Laredo. Páncho would buy a round trip ticket to Salinas, (purely coincidental) Jalisco, Mexico.

After the thirty days' rest, Páncho called Juan by phone and asked for money so he could come back to Encinal. Juan knew that he would show up, and sent the money by telegram. Several days later, Páncho called our house in Laredo and let us know he was in downtown Laredo. This meant we should go get him, and call Tío Juan to tell him of the arrival. Tío Juan usually came and got him the next day. In the meantime, Páncho stayed overnight in our garage. I later understood that he showed up totally hung-over and tired, and needed the day in our garage to recuperate.

This went on for fourteen years. Tío Juan said later that Páncho was the best cowboy he ever had. Hardworking, always griping, but hardworking and would not take guff from anybody who tried to interfere with the Salinas operation.

In 1972, I was working as assistant district attorney in Laredo. I answered a call from Tío Juan. He had just received a phone call advising him that Páncho had been killed in Mexico. I contacted the Webb County sheriff's office, and asked them to look into the killing. In a day, I received a teletype from the authorities in Salinas, Jalisco, Mexico, advising that Páncho had been shot five times in the head. We never got the details on the shooting, but we knew for sure that he was dead.

After Páncho, there were a series of cowboys and cowboy wannabes, some legal and some illegal. We did not realize it then, but the Salinas Ranch was undergoing the change that most ranches in the nation were going through—farm labor was moving to the cities. Ranch jobs did not pay. The ranch was going the way of the cross-country trail drive. Most of the subsequent employees were not good workers. Some just wanted to get by, make a buck, and did not care to perform well. One of these workers was a man named Lupe. Lupe was a white-haired loafer who worked about half speed. After the day was over, he went straight for Encinal and drank down his wages, then came home to the ranch to sleep it off. The next morning, he went out with Tío Juan and worked until five or six again, then repeated the process.

Because of his drinking, Tío finally decided to get rid of Lupe. He paid him, and told him that it was over, and Lupe headed straight for the beer joint. At the beer joint, he very quickly got drunk, and started imagining that Tío owed him some days. For every hour that went by, Tío owed him more and more money, and he gained one or two allies ready to go to the Salinas Ranch to collect his wages. Finally, about six o'clock in the evening, Lupe and two carloads of fellow drunks decided to make the 3-mile trip to the ranch to collect his "past due" wages. They arrived at the Salinas home, and Juan was just getting in from a hard day's work. Lupe insisted Juan owed him more money, and Juan told him he was fully paid. This went on for about three exchanges, and then Lupe said that if Juan did not pay him, he was going to burn the ranch. To which Juan retorted that nobody, but nobody burned his ranch. All this time Tía Bertha was in the kitchen a few feet away listening to what was going on. When the discussion turned to words of burning, Tía Bertha went to the back room, got her pump 16-gauge shotgun, and hurried outside. As she came out the door, she fired once into the air, and quickly ejected and rechambered a shell.

That was all it took: it was elbows and backsides, getting into the cars to get as far away from the Salinas Ranch as fast as they could. The two cars left, Juan and Bertha walked into the house, glad that the confrontation was over. I got a call at my house about an hour after the skirmish. Tía Bertha asked me to come over. They explained what had happened. It was over, and I just calmed them down. We never heard from Lupe again.

Tío Juan's last, more or less permanent cowboy was a man named Jose Vega. Jose was a seasoned cowboy, and worked like Páncho "Manos Pintas." He too worked faithfully for about fourteen years. His right thumb was missing from a boggled dally several years earlier. His routine was similar to Páncho's, but he was an illegal alien, and did not have the mobility that Páncho had. He worked for ninety days, and then took off for a month. He called when he needed money to come back. However, the pick-up routine was very different. He swam the river just above Laredo, then got to a little grocery store and called the Salinas Ranch. This was the signal that he was back on the border, and Juan and Bertha were to pick him up that evening at mile marker 17 on Interstate 35. It was the same pick-up spot every time. There was a power line coming out to the highway from many miles to the west; he followed the power line to Interstate 35, and waited for Juan and Bertha to show. Jose saw the car creep up slowly, he stepped through the barbwire fence and got into the car that then sped away to Encinal.

Today this kind of a pickup would be impossible, because there are more border patrolmen in Laredo than schoolteachers. Some have said that with Border Patrol, Sheriff's Department, Department of Public Safety, Drug Enforcement Agency, U.S. Customs, and an occasional National Guard unit, we are under martial law. Pretty close, and sometimes it certainly feels that way. Today, Tío Juan and Tía Bertha would be arrested within 60 seconds of picking up Jose.

During the last two or three years of Jose Vega's tenure, he started to follow the Lupe trail. He went into Encinal every night and got drunk. Inevitably, something bad happened. I got the call about three in the morning. The Department of Public Safety trooper asked if I was Juan's nephew. The patrolman told me that he tried to raise Juan, but there was no answer at the house. I found out that day that Juan and Bertha did not answer their phone at night, because they usually did not hear it. The highway patrolman told me that there had been a big accident involving Tío Juan's pick-up truck, but that the driver was nowhere in sight; would I please come out to mile marker 36.

I showed up as soon as I could get there. A big bobtail truck full of produce, on its way to San Antonio, had turned over, and there were vegetables and fruit all over the median, surrounding the truck that was lying on its side. I learned later that Jose was on his way home after 2 A.M., closing time for all cantinas, and drove south toward the Salinas Ranch on the frontage road in heavy fog. About a mile from the ranch, he decided to go back to Encinal and keep partying. He approached a crossover and swung over onto the Interstate and turned northbound back into Encinal. After he got back onto the Interstate, within a couple of seconds the pro-duce truck came upon him and could not stop, swerved to miss him, and turned over as a result.

Because he was drunk, and because he was an illegal alien, Jose kept driving for about a mile, left the truck on the highway, and ran to Ramon Flores's house. Ramon was tossing and turning that night, and was awake; he heard the dogs barking and saw Jose's shadowy figure wandering outside in the yard. Ramon challenged him; Jose spoke up and walked to Ramon, visibly shaken and stut-tering, and told Ramon what had happened. Ramon told him to stay and wait for developments. Jose refused and took out through the brush south toward the Salinas Ranch, 2 miles away.

When I finally was able to talk to the trooper investigating the accident, he told me that he wanted the owner and driver of the truck to show up immediately. I went and got Tío Juan, then drove to Ramon's, where I had seen the pick-up parked. Ramon told us what he knew, and then all three of us drove back to the accident scene. I told the officer I did not know where the driver was. He told me I should search and find him. Tío, Ramon and I drove to the Salinas Ranch and went directly to the cowhand's bunkhouse, and there was Jose in bed, passed out. I woke him and told him we needed to go to the scene, and he told me he was ready to pay for his sins, even if it meant jail. He would go wherever he had to and accept full responsibility. I took him to the accident scene and as luck would have it, the trooper felt sorry for him because he was afraid of being deported as an illegal resident, and all he got was a ticket for not wearing a safety belt, and that was the end of that.

This did not stop his drinking, and after several weeks, Tío reluctantly told him that his tour on the Salinas Ranch was over. It had gotten completely out of hand; Jose did not want to work anymore, and Tío was spending more time getting him out of trouble and paying his bar tabs than working cattle.

Tío Juan was sued because of the accident, but I successfully defended the case because Jose had been hit from behind, which is an almost cinch defense in most cases. The trucker dropped his suit after I presented this defense.

In 2002, I was working outside my house, the former Juan Salinas residence, and I noticed a strange car coming up the lane. When the car approached the house I could see that it was Jose Vega. He had not changed much, although I had not seen him since the night of the truck wreck. He announced that he needed help. I told him I would help him any way I could, and we went inside the house and chatted. He said that he was trying to get into the country legally under the amnesty program, and he needed a sponsor; would I be willing to sponsor him into the country. I told him that I would be glad to. We chatted for about an hour, reminiscing about people we knew in common, then he and his son left. He told me I would hear from his immigration lawyer from San Antonio. In a couple of days, I received a form to fill out and sign. The hitch was that I would have to reimburse the U.S. government for every penny they spent on Jose. This meant that if he ever received aid of any kind I would have to pay. That did not bother me much, until I read the part that if Jose were to receive any Medicare or Medicaid, I would have to pay. This concerned me, because at age sixty-five if he got sick or injured, I would be liable. I felt badly about not being able to help him, but he understood and said that if it could not be done, it could not be done.

After the Border Patrol increased their ranks in Webb County, and the law changed, making it against the law to employ illegal aliens, we hired several men to fill the vacancy. None made it permanently. Among these was a fellow by the name of John Crenshaw. He confirmed to me that this was an alias. He said he was running from a child support judgment issued out of the state of Utah. He worked for about a month. He too became accustomed to frequenting the cantinas in Encinal. One night I received a call from Tía Bertha—something horrible had just happened. I hurried over and listened to the story. John had showed up drunk and wanted his pay so he could leave. Tío paid him. Then he insisted on getting a ride to Laredo. Tío told him this was impossible because Tío could not drive to Laredo, much less at night. Tío would take him to Encinal instead. John started screaming that he could not go to Encinal because a couple of thugs had threatened to tell everyone that he was an undercover drug agent, and that he would be killed if taken to Encinal.

When I arrived, Tío wanted me to drive him to Encinal. I asked why, and Tío told me that he insisted on driving John to Encinal, but that at a creek just north of Ramon Flores's house, John tried to take the truck from Tío. Tío struck him on the mouth, and John jumped out of the truck. Tío thought that he might have run him over with the truck. He wanted me to go investigate. A backhanded lick on the chops from Tío Juan, who weighed over 200 pounds, and whose hands were huge bear paws, was nothing to dismiss lightly.

We drove to the small creek, and there was no John in sight. I drove back and forth and side to side, scouring the landscape. I saw nothing, and we drove back to the ranch. The next morning I saw John at an icehouse in Laredo. He begged me to mail his duffle bag. I did.

Ricky was another post–Jose Vega replacement. Ricky was no cowboy, and served primarily as a driver for Tío. Ricky hung out with a rough crowd in Encinal—reportedly, some gang members from Chicago. At a party in Encinal, one of the gang members killed a man. Ricky was placed under arrest because he was with the shooter. He never came back to work after that. However, several days later, Texas Ranger Doyle Holdridge showed up at the ranch with the killer. He had thrown the murder weapon into the yard behind the cowboy bunkhouse. The ranger found the weapon.

Another employee was one we called Bigotes (moustaches). He got drunk, took Tío's truck, wrecked into two vehicles in Encinal, and I had to go get him out of jail in Cotulla. I fired him, and he filed an unemployment claim. He lost the claim. Another was a man we called Babbas (Slobber). He was a driver, and took Tío out to check on windmills and cattle. Part of the trip involved opening and spreading bags of *mascarrote* (cotton seed cake), also called cubes or jumbo cubes. When Babbas poured cake into the feed bunker, one of the cows licked him and got slobber all over his hand. He asked if there was any problem with this, and both Tío Juan and Ramon, tongue in cheek, told him that he would probably get rabies. That night, Babbas, who was sleeping in the cowboy bunkhouse, woke me and told me that he could not sleep, and that he felt nauseous. I told him to sleep in the main house, and I would take him to the doctor in the morning. After the doctor checked him, I found out that the medicine prescribed was not for nausea, but for psychosis. The man had freaked out thinking he was going to get rabies.

There were many other employees—Elia Perez worked in the house for so many years, and Maria who worked in the house but preferred to work outside with the men. There is still a deer blind on the ranch called Maria's blind. She built it, and got the men to stand it up and anchor it. She would help Tío field dress, skin out, and de-bone venison. There were countless others too numerous to mention.

One day we were driving through Encinal and Tío pointed to a young woman. "Do you see that girl over there?" Tío Juan asked.

"Yes, I do, she sure is pretty," I answered.

"She used to work for us cleaning the house," Tío allowed.

"Well she sure is pretty," I added.

"You should see her husband; he peels the paint off the wall." Tío chuckled, and then added *"El marrano más trompudo siempre agarra la mejor masorca"* ("the ugliest pig always gets the best ear of corn").

I asked Tío about the portraits taken when he was in his eighties. "When Lee Karr came by to take those portraits of you and your horse, for his book *Rope Burns*, why did you decide to use a canvas jacket instead of your nice leather jacket?"

"Well, because we always use a canvas jacket, we also call 'em brush jacket, also they call 'em red bugger. They made outta canvas and have corduroy on the cuffs and sometimes on the collar and the front pocket. Sometimes the canvas is yellow, sometimes its brown, and sometimes its kinda red. 'Course they fade and get almost white. They used to always be kinda red, so they called 'em red buggers. We always called 'em *yompas* (jumpers).

"I had a cowboy once. His name was Fidel Guerra, and we called him Fidelon. Fidelon had a yellow yompa. This week in December it got real cold, and we was out working trying to catch and brand calves, and we all bundled up with the most jackets and clothes we could find, scarves, and cover our faces with bandanas, and put on sweaters under our jackets, and long underwear, and extra tee shirts. Well Fidelon, he came to work with just his little yompa, and we all asked him if he was cold, and he said no he was okay. We all thought he was strong against the cold. '*Que fuerte eres para aguantar el frío*' ('You are very strong to withstand the cold'). He would agree with us, that he was right strong to stand the cold.

"Years later, I met Fidelon at a hunting camp, and we was standing around the campfire talking and telling stories, and I told everyone there how strong Fidelon was to stand the cold, and I told them how he came to work with just a yompa and he did just fine. After I finished talking Fidelon looked at me and everybody around the fire and said, 'No, you got it all wrong, I was not strong against the cold at all; the problem was that the yompa, my jeans, and the shirt I wore were the only clothes I owned in the whole world. I wasn't strong at all, I was freezing, I was just embarrassed to say that I was too poor to have a jacket.'"

A couple of years after Tío Juan died, a man by the name of Ruben Guerra came by the Salinas Ranch to visit. He was with his son Ruben Guerra Jr., and he wanted to show his son around. He said his nickname was Gancho (Hook), probably because of his eagle's beak nose. Gancho and his son asked permission to walk around, and to see Tío Juan's trophy saddles. He walked to the *corrales de leña* (the mesquite pens), where he pantomimed exactly where he was holding a heifer that kicked him, right by the nipping pole, that resulted in him getting branded on the chest with the Salinas "S," instead of the heifer.

He told me he had spent about five years on the ranch during the 1960s working as a rookie cowboy, and that he loved working the ranch, and working for Tío Juan. He talked about Páncho "Manos Pintas"; he talked about the different horses he rode, and about Tía Bertha's Fundillo (the horse of course). He said he finally had to quit because he couldn't make it on $6 per day. He moved on to become a roughneck, and retired after many years of working in the oil field.

He told me many stories about his stay, but he showed much emotion about the night of the skunks. He said that Tío Juan had cattle feed in the horse barn, and it was so much that it did not fit in the feed room, so it was just stacked in one of the horse stalls. Well, varmints started to get into the feed and make a huge mess, so they devised a plan. They stuck a 3-foot stick in the open feed sack that the varmints had already ripped open and attached a little bell to the stick. When the bell rang, that meant the varmints were hitting the feed, and the plan was that Tío Juan would come out with a five-shot pump shotgun and take care of the pests.

About ten o'clock at night, everyone had gone to bed, the windows were open as the weather was cool and mild, and suddenly the bell rang. Tío Juan jumped out of bed, put on clothes, and sneaked out to the barn with his shotgun and a flashlight. Tío got about 30 yards away, shined the light, and saw five skunks having a banquet. Tío fired rapidly and killed four of the skunks, one got away.

By that time, the cowboys were up and behind Tío as he shot. After the massacre, Tío told Gancho to throw the dead skunks in the back of the pick-up so they could go dump them at the trash hole about a mile away. Gancho threw three of the skunks in the back of the truck and grabbed the fourth by a hind leg; the skunk was still alive and sprayed Gancho thoroughly. Gancho screamed and threw the animal down; he ran to the horse trough and dove in, and Tío walked up closer and shot the animal dead.

Gancho suffered one of the worse curses a rancher can wish upon a person. *Que te mea un zorillo* (may a skunk spray you). After the skunk sprayed Gancho he smelled terrible. At the water trough he jumped in and washed off. He jumped out and got dirt and rubbed it all over himself, then he dove back into the trough, then he asked the other cowboys to bring him a bar of soap; that did not work either. After trying everything he could get his hands on, everyone went to bed, with Gancho very smelly. Everyone was laughing of course.

In the morning Gancho said that he thought the smell would be gone or to have dissipated, but it seemed stronger than the night before. As Gancho worked during the day, being around him was more and more unbearable, something had to be done. When the cowboys came home, Tío Juan went inside the big house and talked to Tía Bertha. Tío came out with a tiny bottle of very expensive Chanel No. 5, French perfume. He handed it to Gancho. "Boy you're getting to be expensive; Bertha says this ought to take care of the problem. Bathe real good with that bar of soap, and then put this perfume on."

Gancho took a bath and poured on the French perfume, all to no avail. The skunk smell seemed to get stronger. Finally, Tío Juan did not know what to do, so he took Gancho home to Encinal, so his family could take care of the problem.

When Gancho got home, his grandma knew exactly what to do. She told him to run to Tío Tony's Highway Food Market and get a dozen little tomato sauce cans, El Búfalo brand, with the gold, black, and red labels. When he got home, his grandma told him to take a bath with nothing but the tomato sauce, to leave it on for about half an hour, and then to wash it off. Gancho told me that the Búfalo did the trick. He laughed and laughed as he told me his story, then as he started to get in the pick-up to leave, the old guy shed a tear. He thanked me profusely for letting him walk around and reminisce about his early adventures. He said he would be back someday.

As we returned to the house from a 2-hour drive, I approached the big red barn, and Tío Juan said, "let me tell you a story. Right there, by the barn, see that huge pen. One time, my daddy had about one hundred goats. We used to let them roam around the headquarters. They went out in the morning and grazed around the home pasture all day long. In the evening, they come on in to the pens around the barn, and bed down in the huge pen. They was dogs that watched over them most of the time. If they wasn't any dogs, then some of the men were assigned to care for them. They was always someone in charge of looking out for them. If they did not come in by about sunset, the man in charge of them would go look for them and herd them back to the house.

"Well one summer, the goats started acting funny. One of the goats started biting the others, and cutting them up. Then the wounded starting biting others and pretty soon we had quite a big bunch of them that were salivating or foaming at the mouth and biting, and these were wounded from the bites from the others. It was easy to see that the goats had rabies. They was probably bitten by a rabid coyote, and we didn't realize it until it was too late. We had to destroy the entire herd of one hundred goats more or less. We got out a couple of .22 rifles and started shooting them in the head and piling them up. We ended up with several big piles of goats, of all sizes, *cabritos*, and momma goats, half grown, and full grown, and then we got a couple gallon cans of coal oil, kerosene, and burned each of the stacks. They burned for days. After a couple of days, we went back to the stacks, poured more kerosene, added mesquite wood, and burned again. We did this for about two weeks until all that was left was ashes. I had burned meat odor in my nose for months."

I asked Tío Juan about the three little frame houses that stood by the main house. "Well, they just finally rotted, after nobody live in 'em for years and years. But, the one right by the house, we used it to store corn, and other stuff. One year we filled it with garlic. It was plum full of garlic. Then suddenly we were told that this one fellow that worked for us was acting strange, foaming at the mouth and funny. We didn't know what to do, so we threw him into the house with garlic, and left him in there, waiting for him to die from the rabies. He stayed in there a while, and ate lots of garlic. Know what, he got cured. About two weeks later, we let him out, and he was okay."

On a Saturday drive, we came upon the Las Conchas north pasture. "You see that little opening in the fence?" Tío asked.

"One morning we came up on the fence, and it had been cut with wire cutters. All five wires were cut. The cowboy and I walked up and we mended the cuts, and I looked around and picked up sign that someone had drug out an animal. There were car or truck tracks outside the ranch. It was apparent that someone had stolen an animal from me. It could have been a calf or could have been a deer, or a wild hog. I looked for blood but I didn't find any.

"Years later, I was told that it was one of my ex-employees. He and a group of young men came into my pasture with a flashlight. They walked quietly in the brush until they came up on a group of cows and calves. Before the animals could spook, they shined the flashlight directly into a cow's eyes. They moved toward her quickly and kept her blind from the flashlight. Then when they were just on her, they would shift their light to her calf, and keep the calf blind until they could get real close. When the cow started to get too close, protecting her calf, they would shift the light to her eyes and blind her. Finally, they were able to catch the small calf and tape its mouth with duct tape, then tape its legs with tape and drag it out of the ranch in a hurry.

"Well I heard later who it was and that when they reached the fence, they cut all five wires, and when the boy reached to cut the fifth wire, a rattlesnake struck him just above his wrist. Boy they panicked and took the calf in to Encinal, and hurried the boy into the hospital.

"Like I said, I didn't find out about it for a couple of years, but when they told me about the snake bite and the boy, I looked at his right forearm, and you should see all the cuts and scars. He is branded for life. Next time we see him in town, I'm gonna point him out to you, so you can see his arm."

15

Accolades and Kudos

After Tía Bertha's death, we became aware of how much help Tío needed. With Bertha alive, they put on a very good front; Tío looked and acted strong and independent. With Tía Bertha gone, we found out that Juan needed help with everything he did. We learned we had to help bathe him, dress him, and help with bathroom necessities. His eyesight was very poor and by now, 1990, he had lost muscle tone and coordination.

My brother Abe was the only one around who did not have young children and who was able to take care of him, so the consensus decision was that Abe and his wife Angie would come and live with Tío. We started with a whole string of driver/helpers. They lasted an average of six months. They either quit or we had to fire them, then we would get another one.

After work I hurried to Tío's house, and let the driver/helper/hand-holder go home. Abe and Angie, who both worked in Laredo, drove to their home in Los Botines 20 miles away, got their stuff for the night, and then traveled to Tío's. When they arrived, I was relieved and able to go home to my family. In the morning, the driver showed up and Abe and Angie were free to go for the day, then we would do it all over again.

Tía Bertha died in April 1991, and in late June, I heard that Tío Juan had been named Rancher of the Year by Borderfest. Borderfest was a nonprofit organization in Laredo organized about ten years earlier to hold a huge carnival bazaar at the Laredo Civic Center grounds during the Fourth of July weekend. Naturally, I

Rancher of the Year, Borderfest, Laredo, 1991. Left
to right: Abe Palacios Jr., Maggie Rubio, Tío Juan,
Angela Shipton, Ricardo Palacios, Jessie Hines

agreed that he should accept, and then had to talk him into it. Although he was reluctant to accept, he needed the distraction from Tía Bertha's death and the grief and loneliness that came with it.

The usual schedule for the Rancher of the Year was a visit to the rancher's house by the committee and the media, about a week before the fiesta; a supper at the Laredo Civic Center a few days later; and an appearance at the festival itself.

We prepared for the visit, and Tío's main concern was, what if the toilets won't flush? I bought the steaks, the women prepared all the trimmings, and we hosted about twenty people. The Borderfest photographer took pictures of the barn, the trophy saddles, the horses, cattle, the house, and of course Tío Juan and the rest of us. That evening, the six o'clock news on television had a segment on the Borderfest Rancher of the Year. They showed the horses

Trophy saddle, Horseshoe Inn, Corpus Christi, 1956

galloping around the pen, then the rodeo pictures in the den, and then the cute blond reporter asked him several questions.

She then asked about Tía Bertha, "Please tell me about your wife. How did she like the rodeo life, and living on the ranch for so many years?"

Tío answered in his cowboy English, "she liked it okay, we were married for over fifty years, and she never did quit me. She never did quit me." Not quite responsive to the question, but certainly how he felt about her commitment.

During this period, I began to inquire about his nonstatus with the National Cowboy Hall of Fame. I was curious as to why he was not in the Hall. It was common knowledge that while he might not have been World Champion, he was ranked very high during his era. During his roping days and for about twenty years afterward, Tío Juan was a celebrity in area roping circles, a celebrity around his home near Encinal, and of course in Laredo. Everyone within a 100-mile radius knew of Juan Salinas and knew that he was a champion roper.

As time passed, his popularity waned, and even in Laredo, 30 miles away, his recognition and celebrity began to diminish. The older Juan Salinas got, it seemed fewer and fewer people recognized him. This was natural, but I felt that it was wrong. I felt that he was due more recognition, at least as a permanent celebrity locally. After all, he had been the first Mexican American to break into professional rodeo, and the first to make it to the championship rodeos. Essentially, he was the first Mexican American rodeo champion. He did not win the World Championship, but he made the rodeos, made lots of money, won at many rodeos, and left his mark. He was good, he was very good. We could say he made it to the Super Bowl or World Series of calf roping ten years straight.

I felt that he belonged in the National Cowboy Hall of Fame. I was perplexed as to why he was not already there.

I became a lawyer in 1970, and my practice often included mass mailings and lobbying activities for clients, an activity I learned while working for a friend's oil company. I decided to put this knowledge to work for my uncle.

I called Tío Juan's roping buddy and protégé Toots Mansfield, originally from Bandera, Texas. Toots had been inducted into the Hall of Fame many years ago. I asked him why Tío Juan had not been inducted. Toots related that he had nominated Tío Juan several times, but that Tío never got enough votes. Toots replied that he was not sure why he never got voted in, but thought that it was perhaps lack of recognition of a rodeo star from the 1930s and 40s by the voters in the 1970s, 80s and 90s.

I then asked Toots who nominated inductees. Toots said that any member of the Rodeo Historical Society could nominate a candidate, and he agreed that he would nominate Tío Juan. I then asked Toots who voted for the nominees. I expected to hear that only former rodeo participants or members of the Professional Rodeo Cowboy Association would vote, but to my surprise, anyone who paid the $35 annual dues to become a member of the Rodeo Historical Society in Oklahoma City, the parent organization of the National Cowboy Hall of Fame, could vote. I now had all the information I needed. I asked Toots to nominate him once again.

I paid the dues, became a member, called the Rodeo Historical Society, and purchased a mailing list. I prepared letters to the voting members, making the case for Tío Juan's induction into the Hall of Fame. My family and I stuffed and mailed the envelopes and about six weeks later, we heard that Tío had been voted into the Hall of Fame. We made plans to attend the induction.

In November 1991, in freezing weather, my ex-wife and I flew with Tío Juan to Oklahoma City and attended the induction ceremony in the beautiful hall. The ceremony was perfect, the meal and the stories terrific. I was lucky to sit next to Jim Shoulders, World Champion Bull and Bareback Bronc Rider, and World All Around Cowboy several times. Although Shoulders was considerably younger than Tío, he said he remembered Tío and his brother, Tío Tony Salinas, from about the time that Shoulders began in rodeo. I had admired and been a fan of Jim Shoulders since I was a kid. I remembered reading about the ten or so bone fractures he had suffered from riding bulls, including a multiple fracture of his face, caused by a collision with a rearing bull's head.

I think by then, at age ninety, Tío Juan did not care whether he was inducted or not, but he knew that we cared, and that it meant quite a bit to us. In other words, I think he attended the ceremonies for us. We are very proud of him.

It was nothing special, just a matter of finding the buttons, pushing them, and getting it done. After induction into the Hall, his celebrity in the surrounding area was renewed, and we had a new star on our hands. At times he would tire and tell us he did not want to go on with the festivities, but then he would reenergize, and be ready to go.

A couple of years later, I heard that Dr. Joe Graham from Texas A&M University–Kingsville, was writing a book on the old South Texas Mexican cowboys. I received a call from Cynthia Vidaurri, who was working with Dr. Joe on the project, and we talked about Tío Juan. I gave her some details and she was very interested. A couple of weeks later, Cynthia came to visit and spent the better part of a Saturday with us. She was awed by Tío Juan, took many pictures, and definitely wanted to include him in the book. I do not believe that the book was ever published. However, the meeting developed a friendship between Cynthia and me, and she is one of several who strongly encouraged me to write this book.

About a year later, Cynthia called and told me that Texas A&M University, Kingsville, in conjunction with the King Ranch, was having its South Texas Ranching Heritage Festival soon, and would Tío Juan accept a Ranching Heritage award. Cynthia had arranged for several elderly Mexican cowboys from South Texas to be honored at the roping at the coliseum in Kingsville, during the weekend of the Festival. I accepted and had to talk Tío into going. Once we got there, he enjoyed it. It was a covered arena, and we enjoyed the cattle-penning event. After that event, they called all of the awardees to the edge of the arena, and then asked them to walk into the arena in front of the announcer's stand.

Two or three cowboys were called before Tío Juan, and then Tío's name was called. Because of his poor eyesight and poor muscle tone, I escorted him into the arena. I walked him up to the line, and then stepped behind him, as the announcer called his name again, then elaborated on his roping prowess, his history, his induction into the National Rodeo Hall of Fame, and other distinctions. Tío stood there quietly; it was unfortunate that he could not see the young, tall Anglo cowboy who stood about 10 yards in front of him. The stout young man, blond, blue eyes, wearing jeans and cowboy hat, was hypnotized by Tío. He stared at him, as if he had just seen one of his lifetime heroes. He was truly awestruck. It looked as if the young man was going to cry. He reached up with one hand and touched both eyes, then he looked me directly in the eye and saluted military style; he then puckered his mouth and dipped his chin in a "well-done" nod.

That nod meant so much to me; I only regret that Tío could not see it. Here was a young athlete coming up in the sport, fifty years after Tío had competed; he obviously knew about Tío and was thrilled to be in his presence. I will never forget that moment.

The last award that Tío Juan received was in Laredo, Texas, in 1994, given by the League of United Latin American Citizens, commonly known as LULAC. The LULAC organization was formed in South Texas after World War II to help Hispanics gain ground in education and other similar social areas. It has been a tremendous success, has expanded, and has members throughout the United States. The chapters in Laredo have been particularly strong, raising millions of dollars for education and other projects. One of the projects it has in Laredo is that of recognizing Hispanics who have excelled in athletics. Every year they recognize ten or so individuals. In 1994, among several athletes, including Tony Perez of the Cincinnati Reds, LULAC recognized Tío Juan and inducted him and the others into the Latin American International Sports Hall of Fame. We went to the dinner at the Laredo Civic Center, at eight o'clock in the evening. Tío was tired and not very game. He was quiet the entire evening. He could not come to the podium, and he asked me to accept on his behalf. I thanked the organization and all of the attendees and reminded them of Juan's achievements and the fact that he had roped exactly in the area where we stood.

Decades earlier, the city of Laredo built and operated Washington Baseball Park at the very location where we sat that evening. The Laredo Apaches and others played there. In fact, we were just about where the right fielder might be standing. When I mentioned this, Tío kind of perked up. He had told me many times that he roped at Washington Baseball Park, and that the last time he roped there was the only time that his father, Papí Antonio Salinas, watched him rope professionally. In 1936, Tío Juan had roped a match against Zack Sellers on twenty calves at that very location. To my knowledge, Mamá Minnie never saw him compete, other than at the Salinas Ranch arena.

The ride home was quiet. I think as his life waned we all became conscious of the fact that he was declining, and waited for the moment when he could go on no more. As we drove by the San Román Ranch at mile marker 32, he remembered that part of the San Román had been Papá Antonio's ranch in years past, and that after Papá Antonio's death, about 8,000 acres were sold to the San Román to pay off debt. He also remembered that as a twenty-year-old he and a group of boys and girls snuck off at night and went skinny-dipping in a huge swimming pool at the San Román. I asked him who was present, and he told me that he could not mention names, it would not be proper. "Don't ask me who they were, 'cause I'm not going to tell you. *No soy rajetas* (I am not a squealer)."

Tío Juan is the only Webb County athlete to have achieved Hall of Fame status in his or her sport. The country cowboy from north Webb County did pretty well. I was irked at the local newspaper when they did not even mention him at the end of the century in a long article of the best athletes in Webb County over the last one hundred years. The article listed all the high school stalwarts, certainly the college stars, and a few professionals, but no mention of one of the best rodeo stars of the state of Texas, from just 35 miles north of the newspaper office. I'm sure it was an oversight. Rodeo has never been a very big sport in Laredo. The PRCA has tried to bring in sanctioned rodeos, and they have come several years, but presently there is not a sanctioned PRCA rodeo in Laredo.

16

The Last Years, Travels with Juan

The last ten years of Juan Salinas's life were the years I came to know him well. In the first year and a half after Tía Bertha's death, I spent an hour or so every day in the afternoon at his house, waiting for my brother Abe and his wife Angie to show up. When Abe and Angie showed up, I went home. After a year and a half, I took over night care because Tío Juan and Abe had a personality conflict. I stayed with Tío Juan at night, got up early in the morning and waited for his driver to show up, then hurried home for grooming and breakfast and off to the office in Laredo 35 miles away.

Staying with him in the evenings, I listened to more stories for about two or three hours per day. Then on Saturdays and Sundays, the driver, Abe, and Angie were off, so it was my turn to drive Tío to the various pastures. It was a long ride because he had land leased and owned land from 4 miles south of Encinal to 4 miles southeast of Encinal, an 8-mile trip from one end to the other. Then we rode around and checked fences for breaks, checked each windmill or water well, and made sure the water valves worked properly.

We checked about half the watering holes in the morning and the other half in the afternoon. It was really overdoing it, but Juan could not stand to stay home in an easy chair. He wanted to get out see the cows and to talk to people. After a year or so, we decided that I needed to be with my young family, and Tío Juan moved into my house. He lived with us a couple of years until his death in 1995.

The following are short summaries of the stories I heard during the evening talks and while traveling around from pasture to pasture.

"This ranch did not have a tall fence around it. One of my hunters poached and shot a deer on the neighbor's land, and they got mad and put up this tall fence on my south side here. They wanted me to pay for half the cost of the fence. I told them no. Then they put up the fence and stayed about a foot or two away from my fence. When the tall fence was up, I took my fence down and I gained a foot or two of land here and there. I showed them.

"You see that white bone about six feet up on the tall fence. That's what happens with tall fences. A doe tried to jump the fence and did not make it; she got hung up on the wire. I came up on her when she had been dead about three days. I just left her there so the neighbor could see what his fancy big tall fence did.

"I bought this 400-acre ranch from five people. My lawyer in Laredo, ole Judge Blackshear, fixed the papers. Years later, I got a call from three people that said that they was the owners of the property. I told them I bought it. They hired a lawyer and sued me. I went to court, and all I know is my lawyer told me I won and the ranch was mine.

"You see that little stock tank. We call it the *violín* tank. This guy in Encinal he built it for me with a bulldozer and a scraper, dug it out of the earth. That is what is called an earthen tank, or a stock tank. Then, I paid a lot of his bills, and when it come time to pay him, I took credit for all the bills I paid, and he didn't remember me paying the bills, and he said he had dug the tank for free, for *violín*. In Spanish when something is free, it is for *violín* or *viole*. We call it *La Presita de Viole*, which is what the tank builder called it.

"When Daddy bought this ranch, we had to travel about 45 miles cross country with cattle and mules and wagons, and when I come to this Jaboncillo Creek, it was plumb full to the top. My men and I had to swim across on horseback.

"Right there at that little green tree is where I found that poor illegal alien dead as hell. He had been dead about three days. He was only 50 yards from water. I don't know if he was sick and got water, or never made it to the water. I call the sheriff, and they come and put him in a black plastic bag, and took him to Laredo to bury him. I have found several dead people out on the ranch. One time I even found a woman, about ten years ago.

"We use to call them wetbacks, now they says we shouldn't. That you gotta call them illegals or illegal aliens. Heck we just call them wetback and *mojados* (wet ones), 'cause they supposed to be wet when they swim across the river from Mexico. They swims the river 'cause they got no papers and cannot walk across the bridge.

"This is what we call *La Labor de la Familia* (the Family Field). A family lived here for about thirty years. They was sharecroppers. They would work the land and Papá Antonio put up the seed and equipment to plant the field. After so many years the family, they said they own the land. That did not sit well with Papá, and he got about ten or so men with yellow boy .30–30 rifles and they went and moved the family off the ranch. They left and never come back. Someone said they settled somewhere east of Laredo.

"The owner of the ranch is dead now, and so are his kids. The one that owns it now is one of the granddaughters. That owner was a real rough type of guy. When he started the ranch, he and his wife worked real hard. They had four children, two daughters and two sons. After several years, the wife died giving birth to one of the girls. Several years later, the rancher, he hired a young girl to help with the housekeeping, the cleaning and washing, and such.

"Well one day this fellow got all mixed up, and he raped the young housekeeper. This was a long time ago, and the young girl she was afraid to say anything. So, her didn't say anything to anyone. The old man he kept raping her. After several months, the girl showed that she was pregnant. Several months later, she had a little girl. The old rancher, he wanted to run her off, and get rid of the embarrassing evidence, but his two daughters would not let him. They told him that the young girl was their blood, and they wanted the housekeeper to stay in the household, and they would raise the new addition to the family themselves as if she were one of their full-blooded sisters. They did raise the girl, and she grew up to be a read good woman. Eventually became a bank clerk, got married, and had a family of her own. She was raised as a full daughter, sister.

"Rape was not as rare as you would think. Out in the *monte*, who is going to hear a young woman? How is she going to complain, go to the authorities? If a woman don't got a husband, father, or brother to help her, she ain't got no way of getting justice."

One day as we drove around the Salinas Ranch Tío pointed to the working pens on the Las Conchas pasture. "You see those pens there. Everyone asks me how come the fences are so tall. The reason is that my cows always jump pretty high. Some people say it is because I always work them with my horses. They get to where they jump pretty high, so we just build the fences a little higher than most.

"When we are working cattle, we separate the mothers and their calves. This gets the momma cows real mad. One day we had just separated the calves, there was one big old white cow left in the pen, and we needed to move her out so we could bring more cows in. One young skinny cowboy went in the pen to spook her to the gate to get her out. She charged him with all her speed. The little cowboy grabbed onto the top pipe about 6 feet off the ground and vaulted over the fence. But, he wasn't fast enough, the cow jumped right after him, and just as he cleared the top pipe, her head and horns hit him.

"That young cowboy was very very lucky. Other than that boy, I haven't seen any cowboys horned by cows, but I seen lots of horses horned. You gotta lay 'em down, then get some string and needle and sew 'em up. Then go get the vet real quick. Of course, if the guts are pierced, you gotta wait for the vet to come. The vets are hard to find, so sometimes I just had to put the horses out of their misery.

"I had a cowboy from Encinal working for me, and he was a woman chaser, he had about five girlfriends, and his wife in Encinal knew about them, and did not like it. She was mad all the time. One night the cowboy, he come here to this field in his car, with one of his girlfriends, and the wife heard about it. The wife showed up in a car and started driving round and round with the lights on looking for the cowboy in his car with his girlfriend. Then he saw the wife coming so he started driving around with his lights off, then the wife decided she would chase with lights off, and they went round and round for about 30 minutes in the dark. I thought for sure that they would have a huge wreck. Finally, the cowboy got to the gate and the highway and hightailed it back to Encinal with the wife chasing behind.

"That big green clump of trees is called a *Palangana*. Many years ago some sharecropper decided to have a big party inside the clump. It was shady and had plenty of room to move around. Well this cowboy, he heard about the party, and come a running, but he didn't know that the creek inside the trees is full, and he ride the horse right into the creek, and suddenly the horse drowned. They had to cut off the saddle with a knife. The horse drowned, and they just left him there.

"This is where the old wooden house was, and there was Granny's house. We built this new block house in place of the old one, and we moved in the day President Kennedy got shot, November 22, 1963. Right there by the barn, about 1940, I was working on a one-horsepower gasoline motor, we were putting gasoline in the carburetor, and there was a worker right next to me with a small can full of gasoline. The little motor caught fire and the worker panicked, and threw the gasoline right at me, setting me on fire. I ran to the irrigation tank about 20 yards away and dove in. Thank God, the burns were not that serious, but I got burned and scarred up. Damn fool.

"That big steel pipe sticking out of the ground over there on the little hill by the rodeo arena, that is the flagpole, and is all that is left of the little one room schoolhouse we had here on the ranch. Kids walked barefoot everyday from all the neighboring ranches and from sharecropper camps. One teacher taught eight grades. They called it the Atalaya School. There were several teachers here, and your Momma, my sister Mucia, was one of those teachers. She taught here for about fifteen years.

"I was sleeping right here by the window in the old wooden house one day when our neighbor from just north of us showed up about three in the morning. He told me that he had stole his girlfriend. That was the expression they used in those days, *me robé a mi mujer* (I stole my woman). He was eloping and his soon-to-be in-laws were looking for him to kill him. He wanted to be able to go to the very back of the ranch, about 3 miles in, and hide. I told him to go ahead, and I wouldn't tell nobody. After about three days, he and the bride came back out and they went home and made peace with everybody. They lived happily ever after and raised a bunch of kids.

"Right here under these mesquite trees is where Uncle Zack had his little frame home. He used to sleep with a big old black snake under his bed. He had a little brown mule. When he wanted to go to town, he would hook up the little mule to an 8-foot flat bed wagon. He went into town and had a good time, got kinda drunked up sometimes. He'd point the mule toward the ranch, and lay down in the wagon and sleep while the mule walked home 5 miles away. When the mule came to a gate, the mule stopped. Shortly, Tío Zack would wake up, get off, open the gate, the mule walked through. Tío Zack closed the gate, get back and lay down in the wagon, and the mule kept going until they made it home.

"I had this field planted in black-eyed peas one year, I came out deer hunting in the evening, I saw this huge deer, and I shot and killed it. I went back to the barn, and skinned it out and we make venison from the meat. I cut the horns off the head, and just let the horns lay around for years. Then one day Ernest Lane saw the horns and told me I should get them mounted because it was truly a trophy deer. Sure enough, I got it mounted, there it is on my den wall, and they say it's a trophy.

"I bought these 400 acres here, and because it was next to my brother's land, I offered it to him at the price I paid for it. He didn't believe me and thought I was trying to pull a fast one. He refused buying it. The next month I made a contract with the Texas High-way Department to take barrow dirt from the place. In one year, I made four times what I paid for the land from selling all that dirt, and they drilled me a good water well to boot.

"This whole ranch here was not mine. It belonged to one of my half-brothers. I forget now if it was Jose or Antonio. He mortgaged it to a bank in Laredo, and he lost it. One of the bank officers bought the ranch in foreclosure. It was about 1,500 acres. Then the poor bank officer died, and his family could not keep up the payments. I happened to be in *Nueva Yorka,* or somewhere on the rodeo circuit and didn't know nothing about this. When I got back into town, I got word that Laredo National Bank was looking for me. So, I drove to Laredo, and talked to my friend Maurice Alexander, the president of the bank. He said, 'Juan, when you were gone, we bought a ranch for you. We will lend you the money at a good rate of interest, and you can make the payments any way you want.' It was a good deal, too good to be true. But it was true, and of course, I bought the ranch. That ranch is named Las Conchas (the conches, the shells); because there are lots of big ole ancient oyster shells all over. I bet no bank would do that for no one today.

"That fellow there cattle ranched for about sixty years, and only owned 400 acres. He did not believe in owning land. Instead, he leased or rented about 50,000 acres. Then once a year, he would round up all his cattle. He would hire most of Encinal to help him. There were the cowboys with or without horses, cooks, bookkeepers, anybody that wanted to work for three or four days would be hired. He would round up all of his cattle, separate the calves and ship them, and let the momma cows back out to pasture. There was a big meal every day, kind of a picnic. In three days it was over, and everyone was waiting anxiously for the following year.

"I bought this little 60-acre tract of land. It was very strange. This young rich boy from Laredo, he married the woman that owned this 60 acres. Trouble was she was a cantina lady. She worked in a cantina, and the rich boy's family they don't like that at all. About three months after he married, something happened to the lady, she turned up dead. She had no other kin, so the 60 acres it belong to the rich boy. The rich boy family don't want the land, so they offered it to me, it is right next to Las Conchas, so I buy it. And don't ask me no names, 'cause I ain't gonna tell you nothing."

When driving one Saturday on our rounds from windmill to windmill, I asked Tío Juan about a tract of land that had puzzled me for years. It was a 200-acre tract on the edge of Salinas lands, and it just seemed like it was carved out of our lands, and this carving-out looked kind of strange.

"Tío, why is this tract of land in the middle of our lands? It looks kinda funny."

He replied, "Well, that used to be mine, and I gave it to a friend of mine."

"Just gave it to a friend of yours, how come?" I queried.

"Well, it was a she friend, and you know the saying, love pulls stronger than a freight train, so there, I gave it to her, because she was my love mate. And, don't ask me who she was 'cause I'm not gonna tell you. And don't you tell your Tía Bertha 'cause she don't know nothing about it, you hear? This happen before I met your Tía Bertha."

"Yes sir, I understand."

"I camped out under this huge mesquite tree in 1938. The mosquitoes were as big as *golondrinas* (swallows). They were bad. Right here under this tree is where I contracted to go to that match roping when I won so much money. Right here at about ten o'clock at night.

"Right at this very place is where my brother Tony and I and a cowboy named Lugo were riding horseback chasing a cow. I took out after her first, and then Tony and Lugo went off to cut her off on the left. I pushed toward them from the right. Tony and Lugo were running parallel to each other, then the cow jumped suddenly to the left, right in front of Lugo's horse and tripped the horse and Lugo on it. There was a huge roll, on the ground, and the horse and Lugo went head over heels. Lugo did not get up. Tony and I both dismounted and ran to Lugo. Lugo was unconscious. We tried to wake him, but he would only make a sound. I guess he was trying to talk. I told Tony I would go call the ambulance, and Tony was to stay with Lugo. It took about an hour and half for the ambulance to arrive. Lugo was still alive, and they rushed him to the hospital in Laredo. He died that night. I put a wooden cross here, and it was up for many years. It is probably still up, but the brush grew around it.

"By this windmill and water tank is where we had another school, 4 miles from the one by the ranch. The teacher and I were in love. Whenever I would ride up on my horse, she would see me, ring the bell, and dismiss classes. And don't ask me what her name was because I'm not gonna tell you. The building rotted and disappeared.

"Right here is the Arroyo Los Machos (Male Mules Creek). You know mules are hybrids and don't reproduce, but they are either male or female. A female mule is a *mula*, and a male is a *macho*. It ain't much of a creek, unless it rains, then it gets pretty full and you can't cross it. It runs right through this south Las Conchas Ranch. If you follow the creek about a mile or so west, you come to the spot where the little town of Los Machos used to be. This was a long, long time ago. There was no Encinal. The people around here all lived in Los Machos. Then the railroad came from San Antonio to Laredo, and little by little, the people left Los Machos and moved to what is Encinal today. They slowly abandoned Los Machos, and now it's in the middle of the pasture that belongs to Mrs. Evelyn Parker. Encinal got pretty big. It had a big ole depot, for the passenger train. It had a big two-story hotel, with about ten rooms—right across the highway from the old Highway Food Market. Had lots of cantinas too, and lots of gas stations.

"On that lot there is where there was a row of little whorehouses here in Encinal. A man could get companionship for a dollar or two. There were about six little houses in a row. Today I'm told it doesn't cost anything. The little houses are gone. Right there is the one-room jail we've had here in Encinal for decades. We only used it for drunks. When I was constable I was called one day to a disturbance at one of the cantinas, I was going to arrest this one fellow, he did not want to go, and he promised me that he was not going to misbehave, would I please leave him alone. I left him alone, and then an hour later I got a call from another cantina about a disturbance. I showed up and it was the same guy. I hauled him off to jail. In the morning, I went back to the jail and let him out.

"That fellow that lives there. *Ese debe una muy grande* (He owes a big one)." Tío pointed to the big white house.

"How so?" I asked.

"Well when he was younger, his wife got sick, and couldn't get around. He hired a young girl to look out after the wife. After a while, he started wooing the young girl, and they abandoned the wife. She died after a couple of years. Yeah, *ese debe una muy grande.*

"This fellow here, he's dead now, but he came to Encinal without a penny in his pocket, and started farming and ranching. He worked real hard, and after thirty years, he owned 20,000 acres. When he died, he was a rich, rich man. Then his kids got rid of it slowly, but surely. It is all gone now. *No sabe uno para quien trabaja* (One doesn't know for whom he toils).

"There is where Lolo Rodriguez lived. Lolo was a cowboy, and when World War II broke out, he was drafted. He went to fight in Europe, and he got a medal or two for bravery. He came back as a war hero. I remember he showed me a bag of German barber equipment. Fine scissors, knives, and clippers. Made of the best German steel. We got another war hero too. Luis Soto, he fought in Europe also, and he came home a hero too. Encinal has always had its share of good soldiers that go off to war. Most come back, but some never made it back, they paid for our freedom with their lives.

"We had some kinfolks whose name was Solis, but we was never very close. They lived north of Cotulla. Anyways, one day they come and asked Daddy if they could borrow a team of mules, with the hardware, harnesses, reins, and so forth, and some farming implements. Daddy said it was okay. Well them peoples never brought any of that stuff back. We never asked, but they could have brought it back some time.

"That little house there is where *La Cautiva* (the captive), lived. One day around 1915, the Indians came from up north and passed right off the east edge of Encinal. They stopped there, and camped out in the *monte* (the brush), for several days. When they left they had taken this young girl with them, they kidnapped her. We always called her La Cautiva. Several years later, the Indians came by again, and they brought her back to her home here in Encinal. I never did talk to her, but I bet she got some stories to tell.

"That building there was the James Mercantile. Mr. James had everything under the sun in his general store. On Saturday nights, you should see the place. Easily there were a hundred people walking around in the store. He had everything a family would need. Dry goods, hardware, food, rifles, ammo, you name it. On the very end, they had a drug store where you could get medicine, fountain drinks, and a sandwich."

As I drove on through the red sand streets of Encinal, four or five guinea hens ran across our path. This reminded Tío Juan of the fowl. "Have you ever eaten a guinea, a *coquena*?" he asked. "No," I answered. "They taste just like chicken. People keep them on their ranches just like watchdogs. When you bother them, they raise all kinds a hell. Same with the *pavo real* (the peacock). They scream and holler when strangers come upon the house. Do you know what the *coquena* says when it starts chattering? It says *pá' tras, pá'tras, pá'tras.*" [A slang contraction of the words "to the rear," *para atras*.] If you have ever heard guineas, that is what they sound like."

Tío always joked around and flirted with the girls, the waitresses in particular. When we finished having our coffee and biscuits, he would walk up to the cash register and if it happened to be during deer season he would ask the cashier or waitress, "Do you want to go deer hunting?" To which the embarrassed lady would usually answer a polite "Well maybe." Then Tío would deliver the punch line, "Excepting with me, we go hunting without a rifle." Everyone laughed.

After we drove for two or three hours he was ready for his nap. "Well, let's go on home and get something to eat. And after lunch, I am going to have one of those good ole Mexican siestas." After dozens of times, I was the straight man who always asked, "and what is a Mexican siesta?" To which he readily answered, "*a calzón quitado.*" Which means, with underwear removed, in the buff. We laughed and kept driving toward home.

Driving down Encinal's Main Street we noticed a group of about eight men sitting under a tin shade drinking beer. Tío Juan saw them and looked at them quietly. We drove past, then he pronounced: "Those bums say they ain't got no work because the interstate highway bypassed Encinal's Main Street. I don't believe it. They don't work 'cause they don't want to. The highway got nothing to do with it. Then ole Ramon, he says it is all because of Fidel Castro. He says that Castro figured out the best way to beat the United States is to make a huge flow of drugs into the country. So that is what Castro did, and that is what has us all messed up."

"Is that so?" I replied.

"They was only two restaurants in all of Encinal. Both restaurants was owned by brothers. One was the Tourist Cafe owned by Chato Reyes, and the other the Reyes Cafe owned by his younger brother Ruben Reyes.

"Somehow or other these two guys they figured out a new way to cook *cabrito* and to fry potatoes. They took the potatoes and made big wedges, then batter fried them. Then they took the cabrito and cut it into small pieces and batter fried the cabrito. They called it Encinal-style chicken fried cabrito. They served it with lots of cream gravy, and peoples come from all over to eat it. Peoples come from Laredo on weekends with their families and stay for hours having supper. It is pretty good.

"In 1955, we had something happen that was in the news. Somebody got killed on the highway between Laredo and Encinal. A man was walking the highway and got runned over by someone, and the driver did not stop, it was a hit and run. After several weeks of investigation, it turned out that Chato Reyes had gone to Laredo to party by himself, came back in the early morning, and this guy just jumped in front of his car, and Chato could not avoid hitting him. Chato panicked though, and raced home to Encinal and hid his car.

"After a short time, they found out it was Chato and they arrested him and charged him. A Laredo attorney who used to come up here and hunt all the time, Jack Hornberger, we called him Jack Hamburger in Encinal, got Chato off on probation.

"Both brothers kept running their restaurant until they died. Chato died first, and the restaurant closed shortly thereafter. Then Ruben died, and son Wicho and his wife Quina kept running the restaurant for another twenty years. Even after Wicho died, Quina kept on for years.

"Ramon Flores, Ramon Martinez, and I used to go in there for breakfast every day for many, many years. Usually I would have two biscuits with butter and grape jelly, and coffee. Sometimes I brought my own *pan dulce* (Mexican pastry), and everybody give me lots of guff about bringing my own food into the restaurant, but Quina she didn't care. She was a good woman.

"Yes sir, that was chicken fried cabrito, the national dish of Encinal, with lots of cream gravy, yes sir."

On morning drives, the first stop was the restaurant for coffee and biscuits buttered and lathered with grape jelly. One morning we stopped and the waitress came out and announced that they could not serve because the cook did not show up. We got up and left. The next morning we went back to the same restaurant, one of two in town, and the waitress came out and announced that they could not serve because they had run out of propane gas. We got up and left. The following morning we went back to the same restaurant, and the waitress came out and announced that they could not serve us because they did not have any supplies for cooking, no coffee, no flour, no butter, no grape jelly, and no eggs. We got up and left. On each of these occasions, we laughed and laughed. The following week Tío asked to go back to the same restaurant—he was a loyal friend and customer. The restaurant recovered from its problems and started serving again. Tío ordered his coffee and biscuits. Everything was back to normal.

"That blue building there was the Highway Food Market, my brother Tony's grocery store that he ran until he died in 1973. His wife Lucille, my sister-in-law, run it for another fifteen years, until she moved to Las Vegas to be with her son Anthony, then she sold it."

Some weekends I drove Tío to Cotulla to get feed for the cattle. Cotulla offered new subjects of conversation and storytelling.

"Right here on the main street there used to be a barbershop, right about there. It was run by a gringo. Well about 1940, our cousin Fatty Gutierrez from Laredo he came up for the weekend. He had one of those shares of the Martineña Ranch, through his mother. He was getting a shave in that barbershop. Fatty was *medio güero* (kinda blonde), looked real *gachupín* (Spaniard).

"Well he was sitting in the chair and the barber was shaving him. Had done about half of his face, when in walked a gringo friend of Fatty's and started talking Spanish to Fatty. Naturally, Fatty spoke right back in Spanish. At this time the barber realized that Fatty was Mexican, and he reached down and threw the sheet off of Fatty, and yelled at him, 'We don't shave no Mexicans in here, you can leave.' Fatty was shocked, but quickly gained his senses, and just laughed and laughed and walked out into the street. Fatty talked about his Cotulla half shave for the rest of his life, and just laughed.

"Up on that little hill is where the owner of the ranch died. He was wealthy, but his daughter insisted on burying him right here on the ranch without a funeral and without all the *borlote* (hullabaloo). She asked Ramon and me to come help her one afternoon. We went into the house, and to our surprise, her daddy's body was lying on the table. He was dead. She told us to go down to the gate and lock it. Then we hurried back and carried the body to a hole that someone had dug for her. She told us to put the body in the hole with ropes. We did. She was happy, because she did not have to pay for a funeral. Then she told us to shovel all the dirt back into the hole, and cover the body. When we finished she gave us each a dollar.

"This ranch here has been around for about a hundred years. When they had the World's Fair in St. Louis, or Chicago, many, many years ago, when the fair was over, one of the owner's sons brought back a huge wooden horse about 30 feet tall. He bought it from a whiskey company that used it at the exposition. They tried bringing it by truck, but the horse did not fit through the underpasses, so they had to take it down, dismantle the horse into several smaller parts. They finally got it to Encinal, took the parts out to the ranch, and rebuilt it about 5 miles from the highway. I saw the horse many times. Every time there was a party at that ranch, we go drive out there in several cars to see it.

"The owner of this ranch used to ship thousands and thousands of cows out of Mexico then sell them up north. He became a big cattleman, and had thousands of acres here. I was a pallbearer when he died, and we had a real hard time putting him in the coffin because he was very tall. Finally, we kept pushing; we got his legs in and closed the top, then took him to the cemetery to bury him.

"The old man there that owns that grocery store, he kept asking me time after time to give him one of my hats so he could put it up on the wall. He wanted to put a sign under it that I was a roping champ. I never did give it to him. I guess I should have, but I didn't. Now the store is closed.

"That ranch there belonged to Tío Juanito Martin. It is called the Tecolote (the Owl). I rounded up all the cattle and took them 40 miles to a new ranch by the Rio Grande. It took us four days. We slept on the road, under whatever tree we could find. The crew was about ten cowboys and me, and one of the cowboys was a cook. That cook used to work at the ranch, and he sometimes had to take the food out to the *monte*, the brush, to feed the cowboys. One day the cowboys left him the rankest and wildest mare they could find, they knew that he was going to have a very hard time taking the food out on that horse. When the cook showed up at the outer camp riding the wild mare, all the cowboys were surprised. They asked the cook how he did it, and he told them he roped her, tied her up, saddled her, then took a sack full of metal plates, cups, and utensils, and when she started bucking he whopped her upside the head a few times, and she settled down right quick, then he took the other sack full of food from the other cook and rode out to meet the cowboys. They made him a cowboy after that, and he would only cook on occasion.

"Right here is where you go in to the Retamosa Ranch. It belonged to Tío Alberto Martin, and it is one of the Martineña ranches. I can't remember the year, but many, many years ago, I got a call at home in Encinal from my *primo*, cousin, Pepe Martin. He said that Tío Alberto's wife was on a trip, and had been in a real bad car accident and got killed. He said Tío Alberto was at the ranch, and he had no phone there, and he wanted me to go to the Retamosa and find him and tell him to get to Laredo quick. I went out there in my car, and Tío was not at the ranch house. I waited for about an hour, and finally he came in a pick-up truck, he had been riding around checking on his cattle. I told him the bad news, and he got in his car and drove to Laredo.

"One time a bunch of the Martineña cousins, they had planned a four-day weekend at the Martineña Ranch, the Hacienda. It rained about 5 inches that Friday. Well the bunch they was in four cars, and they tried to get to the Hacienda that is about 5 miles east of Encinal. The cars got stuck after they had only gone 1 mile. Finally, they got one car out, they all piled up in the car, and they drove to my house. Bertha and I were home by ourselves, and all of a sudden, we ended up having a huge party. We all had a good time. The next day they went and got all the cars out and drove back to Laredo.

"A poor family lived there at that *ranchito*. They had a real hard time. To make a little extra money the wife made hats. She would save material from shirts, jeans, old sheets, pieces of canvas, wherever she could get a piece of material, she would keep it. Then she started sewing the materials together to make a helmet type of hat. Any cowboy that did not have a hat could buy one from her for a dollar. I saw *muchos* cowboys wearing her helmet hats.

"That house is where a cowboy that worked for me lived. His name was Liborio. One day Liborio called me over to talk to him. He said he wanted me to go to a ranch about 5 miles north of Encinal for him, to ask for the hand of a girl named Maribel. He said he wanted to marry the girl, but that he did not have the polish to go ask for her hand. I questioned him a little, and found out he was serious. He was scared, could not talk very good, and wanted me to go for him. I went. The man that I talked to had five daughters, and none of them was married. I talked to him for a few minutes, and then told him I was there to ask for Maribel's hand in marriage, on behalf of Liborio.

"When I got back to Encinal, Liborio was waiting for me. He questioned me immediately. 'How did it go, what happened?' I said I asked for Maribel's hand and the father said no, but you could have the hand of Margarita instead. Liborio jumped with excitement, and told me that it was okay, he would marry Margarita. They got married and had a whole bunch of kids."

Occasionally I would say that something was impossible, and Tío would inevitably fire back with his impossibility story.

"Ain't nothing is impossible, heck if Camilo's wife's milk dropped, nothing is impossible."

Naturally, I would ask, "What are you talking about?" The story would follow.

"There was this fellow here that lived in Encinal, his name was Camilo, his wife was named Triunfa, and they had two young teenagers. Well time went along, and suddenly their young fifteen-year-old daughter turned up pregnant. They was real embarrassed, so Camilo and Triunfa they made a plan, that when the baby was born, they would pretend like the baby was Triunfa's and she would breast-feed the baby and everyone would know the baby was Triunfa's and not the daughter's.

"Well sure enough, they hid the pregnancy as best they could, with loose clothing, and so on, and when the baby was born, they told the whole town that it was Triunfa's baby, and Triunfa began breast-feeding the baby.

"They say that at first there was no milk, but that after a week or so, her milk come down, and she was able to breast-feed that baby.

"So don't you tell me it is impossible, if Triunfa milk came down, nothing is impossible. *Si le bajo la leche a Triunfa, todo es posible.*

"I was riding a horse through this high brush one day, and I looked about 50 feet in front of me and saw a huge high rack of deer horns. The deer would move his head slightly to the left then slightly to the right. All I could see were the horns. I got off my horse, aimed right where I thought the deer head was, and I shot and killed the deer. I field dressed him, and threw it on the horse and took it home.

"I roped several deer in my life. It wasn't as hard as you would think. One deer I roped when we were working cattle way deep into the brush country miles and miles from any camp or ranch. I tied the deer to a tree, and a few days later, we butchered it and ate it."

While living with Tío and caring for him, we insisted that he accompany us to Mass on Sundays. He was not too excited about this, but he went. Later I asked him if he wanted to go to confession after many years of being away from the church, and here is the way it went.

"Do you want to go to confession?"

"No, I don't need to go to confession," Tío answered.

"Well I'm sure in ninety-some odd years of life, you must have sinned some at least. Don't you think you should confess your sins to a priest?" I asked again.

"No, I just don't want to and don't knows how anyway," he answered again.

"Well, aren't you afraid of dying and going to hell without confessing your sins?" I persisted.

"When I die, I am not going to hell, because I will have paid for all my sins right here on earth. You think my life was just a bowl of cherries, you are wrong. When Daddy died, I was the one that had to worry about putting groceries on the table. I was twenty-two years old. Then cattle prices got so low we can't make no money raising cows, that's when I decided to start roping all over. I didn't know if I was gonna be able to make money or not. Then Bertha lost the baby she had, and it was rough, having her live here alone at the ranch, with no other younger women around to keep her company. Then the dying started. Granny died in 1943, Mamá Minnie died in 1951 and we buried both of 'em here in Encinal at the cemetery. Then about a year later, my brother Chema he got killed in Mexico, and we had to send for his body. Then Bertha got sick and almost died. Then Tony died in 1973; we buried him at the cemetery in Encinal. Then Tío Zack died about the same time, and he's buried here in Encinal too. Then Bob Coquat died, and Polly left town to go live in Marlin. Then my sister Maggie died, and her husband Henry, then your dad Abe died, then your Mamá, Mucia she died. Then Bertha died, I never thought she would go before me. And then I'm all alone; I live longer than everybody else. I only got you and Cata and Margie to take care of me, everybody else is gone. Then about 1985 I start to go blind, and now I am almost all blind. All of this is lots of pain for me. Yeah I got a few *centavitos*, pennies, saved up but that don't take care of all the problems and pain. All the misery, pain, suffering that I have suffered all of my life will be enough to pay for all of my sins. *Antes de morir, aquí voy a pagar por todo* (Before I die, I pay for everything here on earth)."

Eventually he did agree to confession. A Spanish priest from Laredo came and they talked for about an hour, while I went to check on some cows. He was probably right though; he probably did not need the confession.

He had another way of considering morality and religion. "Well I don't know about holy peoples. I kind of wonder about holy peoples. There are some that go to confession and communion every day. Just like Daddy's sisters, Las Tías Chente and Margarita, they lived four blocks from San Agustin Church in Laredo. They went to church and communion every day. When I rode into Laredo, or when I was going to Holding Institute in Laredo, I used to spend lots of time at their house. At their house, a skinny girl used to come over and visit with my sisters Mucia and Margarita. The girls would go along to mass and communion with the tías. So, I guess you would say they was holy peoples.

"Well every night, remember this is before TV, we used to go to bed early, and the lanterns were blown out. Then all of sudden, here comes that skinny girl to jump into bed with me. Real holy that was. Of course, I didn't complain, but when it comes to holy peoples, I always think of that old saying, *comen santos y cagan*

Juan Salinas at age seventy-five. Courtesy Lee Karr,
Cowboy Photographer, Kerrville, Texas

diablos (they eat saints, and shit devils). And don't ask me no names,
'cause I ain't gonna tell you."

During the week, I worked in Laredo. When I got home in the
evenings I always asked Tío Juan how he was doing. His response
was always, *"no más regular"* ("just regular"), in a slow deep Spanish staccato. My kids heard this response so much that to this day,

eleven years after Tío's death, I ask them how they are doing and occasionally, they respond, in a slow deep voice, *"no más regular."*

Looking back, I can say without reservation that my family and I were extremely lucky to be around Tío for the last ten years of his life. We were able to experience taking care of an older person in our family, and importantly, he gave us a tiny window into history, which we can share with others. We shared many moments. It was hard, but it was a blessing. I realize that had he been truly disabled during these ten years they could have been miserable for him. We are so lucky that it was not miserable, and formed a great part of our family history, the days when Tío Juan lived with us.

17

The End and the Almost-Fight

Tío Juan enjoyed very good health. He was never sick a day in his life, was never in a hospital until his last illness, and still had all his own teeth when he died. His only malady was poor eyesight. A horse never threw him. He only suffered a broken bone when he was eighty-three; his hand was by the trailer gate when some cowboys rushed in a bull and slammed the gate, breaking the middle finger on his left hand. He was in his mid-eighties when he started having trouble with his vision. A trip to San Antonio to an eye specialist revealed that he suffered from macular degeneration. The macula, which is a covering on the inside and back of the eye, simply starts cracking like a piece of old film, causing spotty vision. Sometimes he could not see well; at other times he would shock us and comment on the pretty girl about 30 yards away. He could watch television and see and understand the entire show. When he took an eye exam upon renewing his driver's license on his eighty-ninth birthday, he failed the test. They would not renew his license.

One morning in January 1995, my ex-wife Cata and our helper Inocente were grooming Tío prior to getting him to the breakfast table, and on to his routine for the rest of the day. He suddenly fainted on the bed and was unconscious for several minutes. My wife called an ambulance, knowing that she could not get him into the car, even with the help of others. Juan was always a big man, and in his last year still weighed over 200 pounds.

At the hospital in Laredo that evening, the doctor said that Tío suffered a minor cerebral stroke, and that he would require special attention. He was in the hospital for a couple of weeks, and we had to make a very hard decision—that of taking him to a nursing home: a decision I regret to this day. He was in and out of the hospital and the nursing home for the next several months. The nursing home was grossly understaffed and overpopulated. His teeth were always dirty, they never groomed him, and his water pitcher was always empty. He required lotion on his hands and face and it was never applied, consequently his skin was always dry and scaly. No amount of complaining helped. If I had to do it all over again, we would have kept him at home and hired more people to take care of him.

The last time I saw him alive was late in the afternoon, and he was lying quietly in his bed. He wasn't talking much. I leaned over, kissed him on the forehead, and said "I love you," and he responded, "I love you too." That was the only time in our lives that we expressed our love for each other. The almost exact same thing happened to me with my mother. We expressed our love for each other on her deathbed. Why is that? Was it something cultural, or was it the era into which they were born? I never exchanged "I love you" endearments with my father. To the contrary, my ex-wife and I and our children say "I love you" to each other almost every time we talk. I am puzzled at why it was not always done in the past. I think it was the era; everyone was so busy trying to survive, they forgot to be emotional and loving, *les faltaba cariño* (they lacked love and tenderness).

Several hours later, on June 22, 1995, I got a call at 2:00 A.M. from my cousin Margie telling me that the old cowboy was gone. My dear Tío Juan, who was born and grown before automobiles were invented; who saw the automobile take over transportation; who witnessed man's landing on the moon; who marveled at new inventions, particularly PVC plastic pipes and the screwworm eradication program; who traveled the country doing what he loved best, roping calves, was finally gone at age ninety-four. I rushed to the hospital, and there his body was, lying on the bed. Margie was waiting for the funeral home staff to come and get him. It was so sad; the strong, independent, rock of a man was finally down and out. I had known him all my life, but only really got to know him in the last ten years. In those ten years we bonded; we became very good friends. We enjoyed each other's company. We agreed on most issues and decisions. He paid me a great compliment about three years before he died. We were talking about his health, and doing something or other, and he said if it were not for me he would have been dead years earlier. I cannot take full credit; most of it goes to my ex-wife Cata. We buried Tío next to Tía Bertha at the cemetery in Encinal, Texas.

Back in the summer of 1988, I was over at Tío's house helping move furniture. I was in the den when Tía Bertha approached me. She told me that she wanted me to change her and Tío's last wills. As their wills stood, they simply left everything to the survivor. She wanted to leave that part the same, but after the survivor passed on, to leave half of everything to Margie and half of everything to me. I did not know at the time if she was serious, so I said okay, we'll take care of it later. I did not follow her instructions. A couple of months later, she again approached me and told me that the wills had to be prepared, and that she and Tío had talked and that they wanted new wills. I told her it would be better if another attorney handled the matter, being that I would be a one-half beneficiary and devisee. It would be better for a third-party disinterested attorney to talk to them, to render advice on what to do with their properties.

I asked a lawyer in my firm if he could meet with them. He agreed to talk to them and prepare new wills according to whatever they wanted to do. They went to see the attorney and he prepared new wills. The will ultimately left one-half to me, and one-half to Margie. Later, Tío and Tía gave me the wills for safekeeping. At times as we sat and chatted Tío would chuckle. I asked him what he was chuckling about, and he told me that he was laughing about the wills. He thought that some nephews and nieces would not be happy with the wills. Then he would add, "But I don't have to worry about it, because I am not going to be here, you're the one that might have problems. Ha. Ha. Ha." Little did I know.

Well sure enough, his body was not yet cold—it was one day after the funeral—and I got calls from relatives wondering about the will and when it was going to be read. Reading of the will is not a requirement, and frankly I have only done it twice in my thirty-six years of practicing law. Reading of the will is something you only see in movies. Therefore, I saw no reason to have a formal reading of the will; I simply told them that Tío left one-half to me and one-half to Margie.

The next thing I knew a couple of my cousins hired a lawyer. The lawyer called and told me that my cousins were planning to file a will contest. I told him I was ready whenever he was. In the meantime, I filed the will with the county court in Webb County, to have it probated.

To make a long and unpleasant story short, the will was never contested. As near as I can tell, it was all a bluff.

I have asked myself why Tío and Tía left their estate to Margie and me. The nearest I can conclude is that we were here for them during their last years. The reason I came to Encinal in the first place was the love I have for the land. I love the red sand, the creeks, the sunrises, the beautiful golden-hued sunsets, to me the most beautiful part of the day. Encinal and the ranch kept drawing me like a magnet. I remember one long horseback ride I took with my father. Unfortunately for me, we only had one saddle. J. Evetts Haley, trail driver Charlie Goodnight's biographer says, "Saddles were made for men, the boys early learned the sting of horse sweat in a galled crotch." Well I had a galled crotch all right. But even that wasn't enough to dim my love for the ranch. I was hooked for life—the curly mesquite trees, the cactus, the *lagunetas* (lagoons), and creeks, the wildlife. I was mesmerized.

We were there for Juan and Bertha at a time when most of their friends had either died or moved away. It was not planned that way, it just happened. Little did I imagine that in my fifth decade I would own my grandfather's ranch. For the rest of my life, I'll be grateful for the way things turned out. I can't imagine how much poorer my life would be if I hadn't had the privilege of coming to know and love my uncle, Tío Juan Salinas. In my mind, he'll always be the greatest Mexican cowboy who ever lived.

Index

ISBN-13: 978-1-58544-527-1
ISBN-10: 1-58544-527-4

www.ingramcontent.com/pod-product-compliance
Lightning Source LLC
Chambersburg PA
CBHW021903020426
42334CB00013B/456